HOLY SATURDAY

A Memoir of Loss and Hope

GARY S. HAUK

HOLY SATURDAY

A Memoir of Loss and Hope

Secant Publishing, LLC
615 North Pinehurst Avenue
Salisbury, MD 21801

979-8-9903562-7-6 (paperback)
979-8-9903562-8-3 (epub)

PERMISSIONS

Photo of Thomas Hauk courtesy of Ann Watson.

Contents

In Memory of Our Beloved

Thomas John Anthony Hauk

July 18, 1986 – August 21, 2002

Introduction

As my son lay dying during seven weeks of a long and desolating summer, friends often said to me, "I can't imagine what you're going through." My response, sometimes spoken sometimes not, was that, yes, actually, they could. The imagination is an amazingly powerful and useful medium of empathy and moral connection. It would not take much of a stretch for friends, especially those who knew Thomas or had children of their own, to put themselves imaginatively in my place and begin to understand more fully my experience.

And yet, having lived now with Thomas's death for nearly a quarter of a century, I have to say modestly that, no—they couldn't imagine, not completely. Imagination can carry us a long way toward comprehending the nuances and complexities of another person's life, but it finally falls short of getting us all the way in. Knowing the guilt, anguish, and loss I have felt in the death of one of my children, I believe I still cannot fully grasp the ravaged emotions of another parent who has lost a child. I have some awareness, some fellow feeling, perhaps more than a person who has not experienced that kind of loss. But the uniqueness of each loss makes the deepest sharing of knowledge, the absolute commonality of experience, impossible. The lineaments of grief are general; the shading and colors are individual.

What motivates this writing is the hope that it will help others in similar or even wildly different periods and landscapes of grief to imagine the reality of another bereft heart, so that recognition might clarify the foggy terrain. So that some of the surprises along the way will be less shocking and less likely to leave one gasping. Maybe, too, some parts of this story will help the friends, family, and onlookers who surround the grieving person. What can they say? What should they not say? How should they behave? What possible ease from pain and sorrow can they offer? Should they even try?

That this work has been difficult to complete may go without saying. After all, more than two decades have passed between the death and the book. Wanting to record some of my thoughts and experience in the immediacy of the emotional chaos to make sense of it all, I began to pull together notes and journal entries and anecdotes the year after Thomas died. But I had to set the project aside after a little while. The story felt too personal to interest an audience beyond family and friends, too difficult to tell in a coherent way. And death, even tragic death, seemed too daily and common an experience for my story to stand out from countless other such stories.

Death and the grief it provokes have consumed the imagination of writers since Homer wrote of the anguish of Achilles, and since the poet of Job lamented the unfathomable way "bad things happen to good people," in the words of Harold Kushner. Writing about grief in all its specificity is a genre unto itself and includes many classics, among them C. S. Lewis's *A Grief Observed*; Joan Didion's *The Year of Magical Thinking*; James Agee's autobiographical novel *A Death in the Family*.

Even the subgenre of memoirs about the death of sons has its list of superb works: John Gunther's *Death Be Not Proud*, about the loss of his son Johnny from a brain tumor; Nicholas Wolterstorff's *Lament for a Son*, following his son Eric's accidental fall while mountain climbing; Edward Hirsch's long poem *Gabriel: A Poem*, about his son's anguished life and disorienting death. All are poignant, questioning, rendering the despair and helplessness of a parent looking with clear eyes at the reality of snuffed-out promise. The artistry of these works turns the circumstances of the death of a unique human being into a more universal narrative that speaks—or can speak—to all of us.

This book is not quite like those. It does express grief. It does ask some of the questions that death raises, especially death that is sudden, unexpected, and visited upon a life still young, vibrant, and hopeful: Did I love enough? Am I guilty of overlooking a way out of the catastrophe before it happened? What is the meaning of a life cut short in the prime of youth? How does one honor and remember that life in a way that will make it a continuing blessing to others, to the world? Where is that lively spirit now that the body is stilled?

One difference about this book is that the grief told here first manifests itself before the finality of death closes the door forever. This grief begins before death. This grief takes root while a child is driven in an ambulance to a hospital. This grief emerges and grows and changes across seven weeks until that child breathes his last. This grief then lives on for another two decades as the basso continuo of his father's existence, a low, solemn background drone two octaves below the treble of an active, productive life filled with family and friends and work. Always the grief persists to trouble and interrupt the seemingly regular flow of accumulating days. So, yes, grief is a character in this story, and lamentation reverberates throughout these pages.

On the other hand, and equally important, this is also the story of an extraordinary community of love and consolation. It is the story of how, during one seemingly endless, hot summer, love became focused on the situation in extremis of a young man—really, still a boy—whose passing wrung from the hearts of friends and strangers alike an outpouring of compassion, grace, solidarity, and strength in the face of heartbreaking futility. It is the record of a society of faithfulness that took shape spontaneously and unlooked-for, as people from around the world and from many traditions joined in a hope that would ultimately be disappointed.

The first part of this book is prologue. It sets the stage for what happened to Thomas John Anthony Hauk and his family during the last seven weeks of his time on earth. It tells something of his young life to that point and introduces the disease that went a long way in cutting that life short.

The second part records, through emails and journal entries, the forty-five days of his dying. Hours after his cardiac arrest, I sent an email to colleagues and friends to inform them, but also to ask for their prayers and to share what seemed to be a dire prognosis, not spoken yet by doctors or nurses, but lying in the middle of my abdomen like an undigested meal—a sense that what lay ahead could only be the worst possible news. That initial email was forwarded to friends of friends and colleagues of colleagues; subsequent emails with reports of Thomas's condition likewise made their way literally around the world, until his mother and sister and I understood that we were part of a great web of care and concern, whose strands reached beyond our field of vision but held us firmly in loving comfort. The emails became, then, a way for the "Friends of Thomas" to stay in touch with him as well.

The third part attempts to understand the years since his death in terms of one particular day in the life of faith. For those who profess to follow Jesus, as I strive (though stumbling) to do, that day is Holy Saturday, the day between the Crucifixion of Good Friday and the Resurrection of Easter. But persons of other faiths know this time as well, as do persons who profess no belief in a god or in existence after this life. Holy Saturday for anyone is the day after hope and joy have been brutally, completely, and agonizingly killed, the period after the future has been foreclosed and cut off—not just cut off but terminated abruptly, disastrously, catastrophically, frighteningly, and wrenchingly.

Holy Saturday is the nightmare when nothing else has presented itself as good news to replace the future-facing hope and expectation that have died. It is the period when we are left to figure out what to do after we have descended into hell and have wondered whether we can climb back out. If self-murder is not an option—as it never has been for me, though I recognize its attraction and forgive those who take that route—then Holy Saturday is the time to look for meaning when meaning is utterly elusive. Holy Saturday is when we express whatever meaning we find and say to others who are traveling with us, "What do you think about this way of putting it? Do you find here any reason and purpose for the journey ahead?"

This is my attempt to articulate reason and faith in the face of apparent meaninglessness, with the hope that others, too, will find something here to justify purpose and faith.

The Book of Common Prayer asserts that "in the midst of life we are in death." But here is an alternative thought:

The community that gathered around Thomas Hauk that summer so long ago became relentless in its affirmation that—to reverse the prayer book's way of putting it—"in the midst of death we are in life." In a world that harbors disease, war, abuse, starvation, torture, and all manner of death, we are called to find that center of life where, in the words of the liturgy, "meaning is won or lost." Even as brokenhearted friends and family members mourned the dying that they could see was inevitable, they marveled at the inexplicable beauty woven into that time. Despite the horror and tears and agony and questions and uncertainty, the passage from life to death became an unforgettably life-deepening and meaningful experience. This is the story.

Prologue One

It is late afternoon in July, and the humid heat of the Atlanta summer feels as enervating as a sauna. I am running—plodding, really—through the campus of the women's college a block from where I live. A month ago, just after my fiftieth birthday, I started training for my first marathon, three months away in mid-October. Today I should run five miles, but I will settle for three. Exhaustion, grief, and fear slow me down and make every step a temptation to quit, to leave off, to just walk home.

Across town, in the cardiac care unit of the local hospital, my fifteen-year-old son, Thomas, lies intubated, his breathing assisted by a ventilator. His personality—so much that of a teenager curious about life's boundless attractions while staying close to the safety of family and friends—has been submerged beneath the quiescent surface of a deep and intractable coma. His eyes are closed, his breath regular, his countenance one of peaceful, dreamless sleep. He has lain this way for more than sixty hours already, since I discovered him just after midnight on Monday morning. The image of that discovery haunts me.

Now, each stride along my course feels like an insult to the body of the boy who lies inert on the hospital bed. Why am I not at his bedside now and every minute while he lies there? How *dare* I run while he cannot even wake? How *can* I run, with emotions, muscles, and thought so worn out?

Maybe, I think, this is something like what he has felt as a symptom of his Addison's disease—this fatigue so profound that it weighs down the soul as well as the body and makes going another step seem impossible. I recall the spring before Thomas's diagnosis, when he first showed signs of the weariness that would overtake him entirely.

He was twelve then, and the two of us had gone to north Georgia for a day hike to Amicalola Falls, a state park where the highest waterfall in Georgia cascades down a nearly eight-hundred-foot drop. Two trails wind up from the visitors' center to the top of the falls. On an earlier visit, a year or two before this hike, when he was only ten, we had taken the first trail, more arduous and steep. That route loops for more than a mile to a long staircase climbing up beside the waterfall to a bridge where Amicalola Creek tumbles over the edge of a cliff. A view from the bridge down the length of the falls opens to a vista of the mountains in the distance. The second trail, which we were taking on this spring day, was short, moderately graded, paved, and easy for everyone from toddlers to senior citizens.

On that first hike, up the steeper grade two years earlier, Thomas had led the way, eager to find out what lay ahead and keeping up a running commentary as we went. Like his older sister, Alexis, he spoke easily, fluently, articulately, with a sense of humor tickled by the absurd or the puzzling, and with a sense of curiosity stirred by what was beautiful, new, and interesting. He had asked me what I feared most. Then we talked about how we would want to die if it were up to us. Later still, prompted by his offbeat humor, we discussed which animal we'd prefer to be killed by if we had to choose. Sadly, I didn't record in my journal the answers to any of those questions. I just remember that on that day he had been, as he was from early childhood, energetic, engaged, and happy, neither of us imagining that I would later recall our conversation about death as if it had been a foreshadowing of the summer to come.

Now, though, even on the easier trail, Thomas could go only halfway before begging off, too tired to go farther. Despite my encouragement and my offering to take it more slowly, he simply refused to go on. My exasperation came out. Why would he not just walk up the trail like the strong boy he had always been? What kind of adolescent stubbornness was this? It must be, I thought, the consequence of too little exercise and too much video gaming and television. Or maybe it was just the sheer willfulness of a boy unhappy at having to spend the day doing something he'd been only lukewarm about to begin with. Whatever it was, I felt my sympathy and patience giving way to the voice of authority. Impatient and peremptory, I told him to stay put and not move from where he sat, and I'd meet him on the way down. I left him sitting forlorn on a boulder by the side of the trail while I finished the rest of the climb to the top. Driving home later he said barely a word as he slumped morosely against the passenger-side door of the car.

I didn't understand the implications then, but that afternoon of fatigue and surrender was only one of many signs that something more serious was going on. Signs that none of us who lived with him recognized or interpreted correctly. We didn't grasp that a life-threatening illness lay behind his craving for salty foods, his occasional bouts of unexplained nausea, the gauntness of his otherwise handsome face, the circles that sometimes appeared under his eyes, and the skinniness that went beyond the unsurprising slenderness of a teenage boy. He had always flourished as a child. Now, although he ate continually, he looked like a starving inmate of a gulag. We would soon learn why.

That summer, shortly before his thirteenth birthday, Thomas and Alexis flew on a Saturday afternoon from our home in Atlanta, Georgia, to Columbus, Ohio, to spend a week with their maternal grandparents. Their mother, Kate, and I had divorced two years before, but we continued to stay involved equally as parents and sought to keep Alexis and Thomas in touch with both sets of grandparents—my parents in Pennsylvania and Kate's in Ohio.

That evening, after arriving in Ohio with his sister, Thomas developed symptoms that seemed to point to food poisoning. He was nauseated and throwing up. The first suspected source was airport food; before departing from Atlanta, he had eaten some of his beloved Asian dishes for lunch at the airport. But as the Saturday of travel passed into Sunday with grandma and grandpa, the symptoms persisted. It appeared that he might have picked up a more virulent flu-like stomach bug rather than food poisoning. He was sick to the point of not being able to keep anything down. Chicken soup, crackers, apple sauce, uncarbonated soft drinks, eventually just plain water—everything that went into him came back up. By Monday morning he was frighteningly ill, unable to move as he lay on the bathroom floor of his grandparents' home, staying close to the toilet because of his nausea.

That morning, Thomas's grandmother reached me by telephone to say that they had taken him to the emergency room of Riverside Hospital in Columbus on the advice of their longtime family physician. He had thought that the situation sounded serious enough to tell the admitting nurse that they thought Thomas might have appendicitis. That would ensure that he'd be looked at right away. Thus began two days of examination, rehydration, intensive care, and tests. Many tests. The medical team began looking into every possible life-threatening ailment that could create his symptoms—appendicitis, meningitis, encephalitis, flu, Crohn's disease, hyperthyroidism, and who knows what else.

On Tuesday, his grandmother called to say that he was stable, although he was still weak and sleeping a lot. But the cause of his severe illness remained a mystery as the medical staff waited for certain test results. I got into my car Tuesday evening and drove through the night to Ohio, arriving at Thomas's bedside around 7 o'clock on Wednesday morning. What I found was my son lying on his back, asleep, a disturbing vision of an inert boy seemingly cobwebbed into his bed by an array of wires and tubes and surrounded by beeping monitors. I wept to see him. His mother, who had flown up from Atlanta the evening before, was asleep on the fold-out chair beside his bed.

Throughout that day the results of the various tests began to come in and bring the problem into clearer focus. Soon the doctors diagnosed an illness I had heard of but knew little about—Addison's disease. It was, I knew, an illness John Kennedy had endured since he was a young man. Biographers of Jane Austen also speculate that many of the symptoms that led to her early death, at age forty-one—extreme fatigue that kept her bed bound for several months, discolored skin, nausea—suggest that she died from Addison's disease.

Beyond all this, I knew very little. Over the course of the next week and the following months, in visits to specialists in Atlanta, and through the next several years, as we struggled to maintain Thomas's health in the face of this autoimmune disease, we would learn much more about it. But not, as it turned out, enough.

In 1857, when Dr. Addison—who was also named Thomas—identified the disease that bears his name, the discovery came, as many discoveries do, while he was looking for something else. Addison was reputedly a superb diagnostician as well as a dedicated researcher. He came upon the cluster of symptoms associated with the disease while he was investigating something altogether different—pernicious anemia. Pernicious anemia in some ways mimics Addison's disease—symptoms of fatigue, weakness, dizziness, nausea—but the pale look associated with anemia differs from the look of Addison's disease, which has sometimes been called "bronze skin disease." Observers of JFK often commented on his tanned and rugged look. Likewise, Thomas's handsome face usually looked even more appealing because of his perpetual tan, even in winter.

Dr. Addison discovered that the symptoms of the disease result from atrophy of the adrenal glands, small, ductless glands that sit one atop each kidney. The adrenals produce hormones that help the body respond to stress. The inner part of the gland, the adrenal medulla, produces epinephrine, also called adrenaline, famous for its importance in fight-or-flight circumstances. Adrenaline and norepinephrine—another hormone produced by the adrenal medulla—regulate heart rate, blood pressure, oxygen levels, and sensory awareness in response to stress.

The outer part of the gland—the adrenal cortex—also manufactures hormones critical to the body's ability to function under even the simplest stress—like, for instance, walking up a hill beside a waterfall. Aldosterone regulates salt and water levels as well as blood pressure and blood volume. Without aldosterone, the electrolytes in the body—potassium and sodium—can become dangerously out of balance, leading to faulty electrical impulses in the heart and cardiac arrest.

Similarly, cortisol helps to control the body's water level as well as stimulate the liver. Cortisol helps maintain the flow of nutrients and helps the body respond to inflammation. Metabolism depends in part on cortisol, so it is possible that Thomas's waif-like appearance when he was diagnosed with Addison's disease had something to do with an extremely dysfunctional metabolism.

All of this is to say that the Psalmist significantly understated things when he wrote, "I am fearfully and wonderfully made" (139:4). The complex system of interconnecting glands and organs and vessels and nerves and fluids that the body relies on to keep itself functioning—a hydraulic arrangement of microscopic proportions—is a wonder indeed. I often marvel at the simple fact that some smart people have been able to figure out how it all "wonderfully" works. The fearfulness comes in when the body sometimes breaks down. Before long, we would see just how fearfully made Thomas was.

It was because of the atrophy of the adrenal glands that Addison's disease was at one time principally associated with tuberculosis, which can infect and damage the adrenal glands. Nowadays, with tuberculosis increasingly under control and treatable, Addison's disease almost always appears as an autoimmune disorder. For reasons that remain unclear, the Addison's-afflicted body manufactures antibodies that attack and destroy the cortex of the adrenal gland. The disease first occurs more commonly between the ages of thirty and fifty, and more often in men than in women. Why it appeared in the body of a thirteen-year-old boy will always be a mystery.

As late as the 1940s, when John Kennedy was diagnosed with the disease, Addison's almost always was a death sentence. After an Addisonian episode in 1947, while he was in England, Kennedy was given little more than a year to live, but he was able to recover and begin treatment with a newly developed drug. In 1937, Dr. Tadeus Reichstein, who would later receive the Nobel Prize for his work, and his assistant, Dr. Marguerite Steiger, created deoxycorticosterone acetate (DOCA), a synthetic compound that could replace the hormones lost to Addison's disease. This was the treatment JFK received, at first through injections, and later through the implanting of pellets in the back or thighs. After his Addisonian crisis in 1947, Kennedy arranged to have DOCA stored in safety-deposit boxes around the country in the event of future emergencies, because the disease is relatively rare, and at that time synthetic hormones to treat it were not widely available.

Nowadays treating Addison's disease is less complicated but still somewhat dicey. After the doctors at

Riverside Hospital had identified Thomas's illness, they prescribed hydrocortisone tablets to replace the cortisol his adrenal glands no longer produced. He also began taking a drug called Florinef to replace the missing aldosterone, which is normally produced by the adrenal glands and is required to regulate salt and water metabolism.

The challenge of this regimen lay in the unpredictability of how much hydrocortisone Thomas would need. Our marvelous bodies, when healthy, can manufacture two to ten times the regular level of cortisol when we experience unusual physical stress. Get out of bed in the morning and walk into the kitchen for the first cup of coffee, and your body says you need this much cortisol. Decide to hike up the trail to the top of a waterfall, and your healthy body will recognize that you need a lot more of the hormone to make the trip comfortably. The adrenal glands kick in, and soon the right amount of cortisol is flowing through your body. For Thomas, though, a day of strenuous exercise or a period of intense study might stress his body to the point where he would need double or triple his daily dosage of hydrocortisone.

Unfortunately, we could never be sure whether a double dose or triple dose was enough—or even if having the right amount of the artificial cortisol would do the trick. Unlike blood-sugar levels in diabetics, for which medical science has developed a quick method of measurement, there is no fast way to tell how much hydrocortisone an

Addisonian patient needs at a given time. Laboratory tests to measure cortisol levels take hours or days, and one can only guess whether an afternoon's swim or a day of intense schoolwork will require extra medicine or not. The safest course is to take the additional dose, but that can only ever be an estimate of what you actually need, and overdosing regularly can have long-term adverse side-effects.

In the end, the Addisonian patient—and really, all of us, but especially him—can only live, in the words of the poet Robert Graves, like a butterfly, which "flutters here and here by guess / and God and hope and hopelessness." The hopelessness lies in the knowledge that we are often shooting in the dark. But until July 8, 2002, that word, "hopelessness," had not entered my mind where Thomas was concerned.

Prologue Two

On the Fourth of July, a Thursday, while we were eating burgers and potato salad and other Independence Day food with friends at our apartment, Thomas had asked if he could run the Peachtree Road Race with me the next year. Earlier that morning I had run that 10K—an Atlanta Fourth of July tradition for more than four decades, and reputedly the largest 10K road race in the world, at least back then. I said sure, if he felt up to it, we could start training and getting him in running shape. I wasn't sure how he would fare, given the depleting challenges of Addison's disease, but I thought that if he wanted to try, we would give it a shot.

It may have been that his interest in running had been piqued some months earlier when Sara, the woman I was dating, showed up with me at the apartment after we had just finished a three-mile run. Thomas, who had met her only briefly before, took one look at her flushed face and immediately offered her a seat and a glass of water. She was fine, but his solicitude completely captivated her. When she sat on the sofa, he planted himself right beside her and began showing her the wrestling magazine he'd been reading. Sitting beside her—she was tall, blonde, and delighting in his presence—what young fellow would not want to go running with her? And if Dad came along, that would be fine.

That July Fourth, as we were cleaning up after the meal, he asked at the last minute to go with me on the three-day retreat I was leaving for the next day. I explained that I wished he could come with me, but he was supposed to spend the weekend with his mother, and I didn't know whether the retreat center would have room for one more at the last minute. I promised that the next time I went, probably sometime in the fall, he would come along. The next day, Friday, his mother picked up Thomas and his sister at my apartment, and I started on the three-hour drive to the retreat center.

On Sunday, July 7, when I returned home, I opened the front door and was greeted by Thomas, who simply said, "Dad, I'm sick." His mother had brought him back to my apartment earlier in the day for the week ahead. It was not unusual for Kate to bring them back to my place early on a Sunday afternoon after a weekend with her. During the school year, that gave them time to finish whatever homework needed completing before Monday, and they were able to walk to their school, just a few blocks away. Many of their friends lived in the neighborhood, so it was a convenient place for a lot of their activities. They also enjoyed the pool at the apartment complex.

That afternoon, Thomas was wearing boxer shorts, and, without a shirt on, he looked three or four years younger than the sixteen years he would celebrate in just a couple of weeks. He had never been particularly muscular, although he was energetic and loved to swim and rough-house wrestle with me. In fact, spurred by his amusement at professional wrestling, he had persuaded the high school wrestling coach two years earlier to let him try out for the team when he was only in seventh grade. The coach had graciously found a place for him on the roster. He wrestled in the lightest weight class in a singlet that appeared too large for him; I think he actually scored a win when the opposing team had no one small enough to wrestle him and defaulted the bout. In the past year he had had to leave the team because his illness made him too weak to wrestle, despite the encouragement of his teammates. (That entire team, along with the coach, would come to his memorial service.)

Now, his thin frame stood before me as I tried to size up the situation after just walking in the door. He said that he had been eating soup and his favorite ramen noodles (heavy in sodium, which he always seemed to crave) but was unable to keep anything in his stomach. Often, in the past, symptoms like these—persistent nausea, weakness, inability to eat anything—had prompted trips to the emergency room at the local children's hospital, where he would be given an IV drip to replenish his depleted electrolytes. As that Sunday afternoon lengthened into evening, I weighed whether another trip to the hospital was in order. In the end, we decided to wait and see how Thomas felt in the morning. I tucked him into bed around 10 o'clock, and when I looked in on him around 11:30 that night, he was awake. I kissed him and told him I loved him.

The sound that woke me an hour or so later was like nothing I had ever heard before—a low, regular rasping, like the sound of a ripsaw being drawn slowly through the length of a board every few seconds. What it was I could only guess. How long it had been going on I didn't know. Swimming up out of a deep sleep, I had to take a moment before I realized that the noise was coming from Thomas's bedroom.

Fear took hold of me. What was happening? I threw off my covers and stepped quickly to his room, where I flipped on the wall switch for the ceiling light. What I saw stunned me. Thomas lay stretched out uncovered, unconscious, but gasping in some kind of apparent involuntary reflex. His body was trying, in its autonomic self-defense—what I would later hear called agonal breathing—to suck in air and try to stay alive.

Rushing to his bedside, I shouted at him and slapped his face to try to wake him. No response. No pulse. I ran for my phone and called 911 for an ambulance. I shouted to Alexis, who was sleeping in the room next door. Bleary-eyed, startled, she walked out of her room to a scene of horror and began to cry.

As the female 911 dispatcher sent out the call to the fire department, which was less than three blocks from our apartment, she guided me through the steps of CPR. Following her instructions, I lifted Thomas off his bed and laid him on his back on the floor. I put my mouth to his and blew air into his lungs. I felt his chest rise as my breath filled his lungs. Then I pushed violently and swiftly ten times over his heart before filling his lungs again with my breath and repeating the pressure on his heart. This I continued until the EMTs arrived.

Within minutes, it seemed, they were at the door, and Alexis let them in. I moved out of the way as they took over and began to try to revive Thomas. Remembering the scene now, all these years later, I see two youngish men and a young woman ranged around his prone figure, their emergency kits open, vials and needles and tubes spread out on the floor, gauze pads, packages ripped open. Somewhere in the mix there was probably a defibrillator. They asked Alexis and me to leave the room and give them space to work. More than that, I suspect, they probably had recognized immediately the direness of the situation and wanted to work without our emotions in the way.

Minutes passed. Alexis and I had gone to the living room to wait—and to pray. I felt without a doubt in my mind or heart that Thomas was dead. Or nearly so. Not likely to make it out of the apartment with soul and body together. I felt as if the world had become a Dali painting,

"The Persistence of Memory," in which reality not only was melting around me but also was erasing all the coordinates by which I regularly made my way forward through the days. And yet my prayer—maybe blasphemous, no doubt presumptuous, certainly audacious—was this: "God, you brought your own son back from the dead. Give me mine back." If God could resurrect a crucified, dead, and buried Jesus, surely an unconscious boy in his bedroom could come back to lively wakefulness.

Half an hour went by, then another half hour, and during that time I kept checking with the emergency team to see what was happening. They were working quietly but intensely and quickly. The lead technician kept assuring me that they were doing everything they could to bring Thomas back to consciousness.

At last, surprisingly, they said they were ready to take him by ambulance to the hospital. They had lifted him onto a stretcher and were preparing to take their precious cargo out the door. Here was an opening. Here was hope. Would he be okay, I asked. They were doing everything they could, came the noncommittal answer.

As they maneuvered their way out the door, they admonished me not to follow too closely in my car, but they said they'd be going to DeKalb Medical Center, just two miles away. Feeling the need for pastoral company and prayer, I called an old friend, the chaplain at Emory University, and asked her to meet Alexis and me at the emergency room. Alexis called a school friend whose parents also were great friends, and they said they, too, would set out to meet us at the hospital. It was after 1 a.m.

By the time we all were gathered in the waiting room of the emergency department, Thomas had been delivered by the ambulance crew and was somewhere back in the bowels of the hospital, under the care of doctors and nurses. We had no indication of what they were doing, no idea what to expect. But I, who had held my son's limp body and had seen his otherwise inert lungs and chest rise as I breathed my breath into him—I expected the worst.

Letters While My Son Is Dying

Monday, July 8, 2002, 11:15 a.m.

Dear Friends,

Please forgive this broadcast email to you, but I'm writing to ask for your urgent prayers and good thoughts for Thomas. Early this morning, around 12:45, he nearly died of cardiac arrest after suffering through an apparent crisis caused by his chronic adrenal failure.

He's in the cardiac care unit of DeKalb Medical Center on a ventilator, being attended by nurses and doctors who have shown marvelous compassion and earnest attention. What he really needs is courage, love, mercy, God's healing—and time for him to come back from wherever it is he has gone. While his body lies before us in the hospital bed, his breath rising and falling with the ventilator, the boy himself is mysteriously absent. The doctors have given us reason to hope for the best, but nothing is certain at this point, and much is simply unknown. All is being done that can be done, but what you could add is hope and faith, which I struggle to hold onto just now.

Gary

Tuesday, July 9, 8:56 p.m.

Dear Friends,

Again, I hope you will pardon the email, but this seems the best way to bring all of you up to date on Thomas's condition. First, I have to say that Thomas, his mother and sister, and I have been overwhelmed by the love and support we have felt from you and countless others since the early morning hours yesterday, when Thomas's ordeal began. I have tried to thank each of you individually as you've come by the hospital or called or sent emails. But know, once again, that your presence in our lives means more than we can ever fully express. Thomas's room has been filled with an outpouring of prayer and kindness unlike anything I've ever experienced, and if Buddhists, Episcopalians, Methodists, Lutherans, Baptists, Unitarians, Jews, Muslims, and Catholics all praying in the same hundred square feet can effect a miracle, then I am looking for one.

Frankly, a miracle is needed. Thomas's cardiopulmonary condition has improved since yesterday, and the medical staff are happy with that development. His vital signs are strong; his heart was apparently undamaged by the cardiac arrest; his tests indicate a very good base from which to improve.

The big piece of the puzzle that remains blank, mysterious, and extraordinarily important is what's happening in his brain. He is in a deep coma. Since yesterday afternoon, he has shown almost no response to external stimuli—tickling and scratching of the feet, lights shined into his pupils, gentle pin pricks on the arm. The EEG from this morning indicates very slow brainwave activity, although it is encouraging that there is activity. Both of the neurologists who saw him today, however, are less than encouraged by the fact that he has not become more responsive in the critical two days since his heart stopped pumping oxygen to his brain. Still, it seems too early to come up with a solid prognosis.

What's clear is that the Thomas who took his leave Sunday night/Monday morning is not yet present in his room at the hospital. Looking at my son on his hospital bed, I don't know where that charming and exasperating and funny young man has gone. But it's also clear that we still have Thomas with us to love, and for that we are inexpressibly grateful. We are still figuring out how best to love him day by day in his present condition, and in some sense that's a gift—to be able to see our son, our brother, our friend, for who he is in this moment and to care for him with all that we can give him.

Thank you for your gifts to him and to us as well.

Gary

Letters from friends

Wednesday, July 10

Dear Gary,

News has reached us here in Switzerland of Thomas's illness. Please know that we are thinking of all of you and our prayers are with you.

May I offer two pieces of advice:

1- Stand in the room with Thomas and, even if he is in deep coma, close your eyes and open yourself to his presence. You will be able to be "in touch" with him.

2- I remember a case of a young man in a deep coma. I asked the head neurologist what the prognosis was and what one does. He said that no one knew what the prognosis is on a young patient in a coma and that one did nothing; one just waited. A couple of months later, the young man woke up and spent the summer on a construction job. So, do not let the doctors or your own discouragement lead you to despair. Wait patiently in the Lord.

Much love.
D B

* * *

Gary—

In that greying and mysterious place . . . we have heard from all of our foremothers and forefathers in the faith, there is Presence . . . or as Teresa said, I have been to the bottom of the pit and it is firm . . . and we are all there with you.

Love.
B P

* * *

Gary,

My prayers are going up because I have faith and belief in a miracle-working God. My thoughts are with you because I feel your pain. The pain of dealing with such profound grief, to have your whole life changed in an instant, to find yourself in a world that you don't recognize. The pain of not being able to make things better right now for Thomas.

Gary, as you go through this journey, you do whatever feels right to do. There are no rules.

One of the scriptures that I read which provided comfort was Habakkuk 3:17-19 (The Hymn of Faith):

Though the fig tree may not blossom,
Nor fruit be on the vines;
Though the labor of the olive may fail,
And the fields yield no food;
Though the flock may be cut off from the fold,
And there be no herd in the stalls,
Yet I will rejoice in the Lord,
I will joy in the God of my salvation.

The Lord God is my strength;
He will make my feet like deer's feet,
And He will make me walk on my high hills.

Give Thomas a hug for me.

Agape.
C B

Thursday, July 11, 12:01 a.m.

Dear Friends:

So many of you have e-mailed questions or expressions of support and love, so I want to give you just a brief report on where things stand with Thomas tonight.

Not much has changed since yesterday. Despite hope that he would be able to come off the ventilator today, he continues to run a fever that indicates some kind of infection, and until that infection is cleared up and the fever goes down, the pulmonologist does not want to risk leaving Thomas to fend for himself without the support of the ventilator.

He continues to be deeply in coma. We are preparing for a long sojourn in the hospital.

In some ways—now near the end of the third day since Thomas's cardiac arrest—this situation feels like it is just beginning to get hard. The immediate crisis has been met, but the journey from here is calling, impossibly, for deeper reserves of hope and strength. Thank you for all you have done to point the way to those reserves.

Peace,
Gary

Letters from friends, Thursday, July 11

Dear Gary:

Never apologize for your updates, nor curtail them until Thomas is once again an up-and-running, mercurial teenager.

Once Thomas does wake up, he will have a lot of explaining to do. How, for instance, did Thomas steal the concern and affection of my mother, 104 miles away from Atlanta? I have been told to call her every day with an update, and I have. Similarly, how did he get on the list of concerns of my sister, who is raising two children of her own in Cincinnati? For her, I offer frequent email updates.

For months now, I have been mourning the fact that my beloved Siberian husky has liver cancer. There had seemed room in my heart for no being beyond her sweet, gentle self. I now find that someone has taken a chalk mark and equally divided a heart that already seemed full. So, keeping Thomas company now—as he debates his departure and arrival points—is a beautiful canine companion who is steadfast, quiet, shy, and a source of tremendous tranquility. I assure you that she will steer him in the right direction; she always has done so for me.

S C

Thursday, July 11, 4:38 p.m.

Dear Friends,

Thomas has seemed to be a bit responsive today. My friend Bill was massaging Thomas's feet this morning and noticed that his toes were wiggling, and when I began to tickle

Thomas's feet, they started twitching. Was it a reflexive response or just the fever? An anthropologist friend who visited a couple of days ago reminded me of a classical anthropological question—when is an eye twitch just a twitch, and when is it a wink? I don't know what Thomas's twitching feet meant, exactly, but I'm hanging onto every quark of hope that comes along. For me, the twitch was a wink.

When I have looked on my son over the past few days, I have not been able to say just where that young man's spirit has gone for now. And I suppose for that reason the passage from the Psalms that has come to mean the most to me over the past three days is from Psalm 139. Wherever Thomas is—and in important ways he is still, wonderfully and mysteriously, in that hospital room—he is surrounded by the love and care of God as well as the love and care of family and friends and people he's never met.

A time of gathering to pray for Thomas is being offered at the Episcopal Church of the Epiphany this evening. There will be an opening and a closing prayer, but beyond that the time will not be a structured service—more a period of silent communing in hope and faith for anyone who wishes to come and pray together. People of any faith will be welcome, and all may come and go as they need to.

Come if you can. But if you can't, please know that I know you are praying with us.

Psalm 139

[7] Whither shall I go from thy spirit? or whither shall I flee
from thy presence? [8] If I ascend up into heaven, thou art
there: if I make my bed in hell, behold, thou art there. [9] If I
take the wings of the morning, and dwell in the uttermost
parts of the sea; [10] Even there shall thy hand lead me, and
thy right hand shall hold me. [11] If I say, Surely the darkness
shall cover me; even the night shall be light about me.
[12] Yea, the darkness hideth not from thee; but the night
shineth as the day: the darkness and the light are both alike
to thee.

[13] For thou hast possessed my reins: thou hast covered
me in my mother's womb. [14] I will praise thee; for I am
fearfully and wonderfully made: marvellous are thy works;
and that my soul knoweth right well. [15] My substance was
not hid from thee, when I was made in secret, and curiously
wrought in the lowest parts of the earth. [16] Thine eyes did
see my substance, yet being unperfect; and in thy book all
my members were written, which in continuance were
fashioned, when as yet there was none of them.

[17] How precious also are thy thoughts unto me, O God!
how great is the sum of them! [18] If I should count them, they
are more in number than the sand: when I awake, I am still
with thee.

Gary

Letters from friends

Friday, July 12

Gary,

I was one of the people who came to the church last night, and the prayers and concern in the room seemed almost palpable. I couldn't see if you were there, but I hope you felt it. I hope Thomas felt it. You should count among the many things you have given your children the community of love you have built around them over the years.

I too choose hope from your account.

As always, many good wishes and prayers.

S W

* * *

Friday, July12, 6:42 a.m.

I was moved to tears this morning by the faith you have found in the Psalms. My mother keeps a copy of the Psalms by her bed. It is worn with use. It has helped her through bad times and been her rock and her shield on so many occasions. May these Psalms continue to help you and, with the help of the One in the

Heavens Above, may the Psalms one day be the vehicle through which you give voice to your rejoicing over Thomas's recovery. And so may it come to pass.

Shalom.
D L

* * *

Gary,

Thank you for the privilege of allowing me to see Thomas today. There's something about this kid, abled or not, that draws people to him. He moved his toes, swallowed a few times and shifted his eyes. Not sure if this is reflex or a signal that he's coming back to us, but it was gratifying to witness. I'm holding on to God's promises.

Gary, I know it's difficult to let people know when you need things, because you're really not sure what you need. I suppose that doing your own stuff is also a way to stay in tune to reality as you knew it before this unfamiliar experience. I know you're not helpless; however, if you need anything, let your friends know. We're all here to help.

Peace and Love.
C B

Saturday, July 13, 12:32 a.m.

Dear Friends,

If I don't respond personally to each of your e-mails, know that I have read them all and have been deeply touched and redeemed by every one of them. They are an amazing outpouring of encouragement, profound hope, occasional humor (important), stimulus to sudden tears, memories that stir laughter, practical wisdom, and insight. You are an astonishing, good community, bound together in ways that you don't fully know yourselves (any more than I do). Thomas and his family are blessed far beyond deserving to be a part of you.

Today (Friday) Thomas's temperature has gone down, and the pulmonologist continues to be hopeful that things will stabilize enough for them to get our boy off the ventilator Saturday or Sunday. The neurologist observed the foot twitchings and thought them interesting enough to order another EEG, to see whether there's some brain activity that can be correlated to them. The twitching may be merely autonomous response to the fever, or it may be a sign of something better. We'll see.

Otherwise, things remain much the same. The situation offers many difficulties, not the least being that those who are close to Thomas have been ushered into a place where our grief cannot be consummated.

Thomas is gone and not gone—as if asleep, but unwakeable. The mystery of personality confronts us in its utter quiescence. I hope with everything in me for Thomas's speedy return, while having only guesses about what he's up to, and where he has gone, or what it would mean to him to come back. (I think of Lazarus emerging from the tomb: What did the light of the sun feel like after the darkness of death? Nikos Kazantzakis, in *The Last Temptation of Christ,* imagined Lazarus sorry to have returned from the tomb, weary in a body that no longer thrives, longing for a return to the peace of death. I cannot believe that Thomas would want that.)

These lines from "East Coker," in Eliot's *Four Quartets,* have been part of my spiritual arsenal for more than two decades, but they have never hit home quite as palpably as now.

> *I said to my soul, be still, and wait without hope*
> *For hope would be hope for the wrong thing; wait without love*
> *For love would be love of the wrong thing; there is yet faith*
> *But the faith and the love and the hope are all in the waiting.*
> *Wait without thought, for you are not ready for thought:*
> *So the darkness shall be the light, and the stillness the dancing.*

For now, the only thing we seem able to do is to maintain this vigil, letting Thomas bide his time and determine where and how he wants to do his dancing.

Peace and love to you all.
Gary

Sunday, July 14, 11:24 p.m.

Dear Friends:

Just a brief note. The EEG ordered yesterday was not done, for reasons obscure to me, and this has led his mother to deliver a good, appropriate, and stern lecture to a neurologist. Apparently, according to the nursing staff, such lectures to doctors are something that must be done from time to time to maintain the karmic balance of the universe.

The main thing is that we all want to see some signs of Thomas beginning to wake from his deep, deep tuning out from all that's going on around him (so like a teenager). I thought it was hard to get him to take out the garbage. Getting him to wake up right now makes the garbage seem trivial.

This afternoon, I was folding some laundry that had sat in the basket since last Sunday evening. Most of it was his—shorts and tee-shirts that he had worn once (in some cases for a matter of mere hours) before throwing them in the hamper.

As I folded, I realized that he and I have khaki shorts that are almost identical. The difference is that, on mine, the button at the waist is unbuttoned while in the laundry, and on his the button is buttoned. And on every pair of his shorts—four or five—the button was buttoned. This is not a function of his being meticulous—taking off the shorts and buttoning the button before throwing them in the hamper. No, it's a matter of his being so skinny that he could slip his pants over his slender waist and hips without unbuttoning or even, in most cases, unfastening his belt!

Okay—some good news: on his admission to the hospital he weighed 110 pounds (at five feet eight and a half inches). Yesterday, after a couple of days of feeding through a tube, he was up to 116. I'll take it!

Peace and love to you.
Gary

Letter from a friend, Sunday, July 14

Dear Gary—

We returned home from Italy on Friday evening, and on Saturday I began to wade through the email. I was so devastated to find yours. Although I know nothing of Thomas,

I know about what the suffering of kids does to parents. I can't fully imagine what you are going through, hanging between two worlds—hoping yet experiencing the deepest terror and grief.

This morning's lectionary readings—Romans 8:18–23. Since I was the reader this morning, I got to think about them well in advance. And as I read them, I prayed them for you and your Thomas. It's Paul on the sufferings of this present time, the futility of creation, the freedom of the children of God, but especially the groaning as we wait.

What makes this time so difficult is the unclarity, the waiting, the hoping that seems hopeless. But this is the human condition, only you are experiencing it in its pure, unrelieved form. Gary, please know that we are with you. And that I am praying for you and your skinny kid. In the end, God is merciful, but none of us feel that mercy now.

Wordsworth is running through my mind, and his lines have often given me solace—

There is a comfort in the strength of love
which makes a thing endurable
which else would overset the brain
or break the heart.

Your years of parent love will come to your aid.

Sending blessings.
D G

Journal Entry, Sunday, July 14

This week has made me think how good it would be if we could treat all of life as critical care. What if we could give to everyone around us the kind of care and attention that Thomas has received moment by moment in the hospital? That kind of focused, faithful, intentional, healing attentiveness seems to me to be what the Gospels attribute to Jesus. But I think we ordinary mortals would go insane trying to be so diligently and fully attentive to every person every minute. Every moment would present an existential crisis, a choice between self-preservation and selfless emptying. We have to find ways to anesthetize ourselves against the harsh realities that are all around us.

Letter from a friend, Sunday, July 14

Dear Gary,

My mother called me and said she said a "misha berra." I was completely befuddled and asked her what she meant. She told me that a misha berra was a special Jewish prayer for healing. I told her I knew WHAT it was, I just didn't know WHO it was for. She said, "It's for your friend's son, the one you asked me to pray for." I said, "Mom, his name is Thomas." She told me that God knew who she meant.

There you go, special prayers to God . . . from Boynton Beach, Florida.

Here's a hug!
D L

Monday, July 15

Dear Friends:

Today a setback of sorts but also a sign, perhaps, of better things to come.

Through late Saturday night and early Sunday morning, Thomas's heart rate dropped below forty beats a minute, and the nurses gave him atropine to stimulate his heart. The cardiologist had little insight for us about what caused the slow rate, unfortunately.

The hopeful sign—during most of the day today Thomas had his eyes open, staring vacantly, his eyelids unblinking. About 3 o'clock this afternoon, I put myself where I thought he would be looking if he were focusing. I stared straight into his eyes and said, "Thomas, can you blink your eyes?" His eyelids—which hadn't moved all day—went down a quarter of a blink. This was downright eerie. I said it again—"Thomas, blink your eyes again"—and the eyelids went down again, not all the way closed, but perceptibly and on cue. About an hour later I repeated this with the same results: two requests, two blinks.

The puzzler is that in the seconds after those responses, his eyelids blinked a couple more times without cues, so I'm wondering whether the first blinks were odd coincidence and really the result of random neuron firings, or were purposefully responsive.

I'm going with "purposefully responsive."

Thursday is Thomas's sixteenth birthday, and we are contemplating what kind of celebration might be appropriate. Come what may, we intend to celebrate the birth of our boy, who was delivered by cesarean section at 8:36 a.m. on July 18, 1986. It was maybe a preview of things to come, that he had apparently done a somersault on the way to the hospital and arranged himself for a butt-first arrival. Thanks for the complication!

Truly, though, we are glad for his birth, grateful for his life, and joyful that he is still with us. We might push the nurses' limits a bit (sweet Nurse Joyce, who looked after him all day today, blanched when I asked what kind of celebration would be permitted). But we're going to do something to mark the day. If nothing else is possible, please remember Thomas with a prayer on the 18th (as I know you will do anyway).

Love to you all.

Gary

Tuesday, July 16, 7:35 a.m.
Thomas at 16-minus-two-days

Dear Friends:

Just a quick note. Yesterday, Thomas's temperature remained normal through the day, going up briefly to 100.2 before I left at 9 last night. The plan is to take the ventilator tube out of Thomas sometime today. This would alleviate some physical stress. Better still, it would bring that handsome face out from behind the mask of tape that holds the tube in place.

Thomas was not able yesterday to repeat the blinking feat of Sunday, but there were other signs of responsiveness: his heart rate rose into the high-50s during a couple of his favorite music CDs (Run-DMC and the *Saturday Night Fever* soundtrack—go figure), and his arms appeared to move in response to his grandfather's voice.

With the instruction of two physical therapists under our belts, his mother and I are now "going to the gym" with Thomas several times a day—moving his arms and legs in various ways to keep the joints limber and the muscles somewhat toned.

The most difficult thing right now is also, in some ways, the easiest—waiting: difficult because it leaves us in complete uncertainty, easy because it's all we can do, in addition to praying.

One of you reminded me the other day of Psalm 27, the last verse of which reads, "Wait for the Lord, be strong, and let your heart take courage." There is waiting for Godot, but then there is waiting for the Lord. In this latter kind of waiting, we know at least what we are waiting for—God's mercy.

Peace.
Gary

Journal Entry, Tuesday, July 16

The ambiguity of this time we are in. I am reminded of a story Kate told about Thomas and the church she serves as assistant minister. When Thomas and Alexis are staying with her, they go together to services and events there. Like many churches, this one hosts a weekly evening meal that brings together people of all ages—families, widows, widowers, young singles. After the meal, if you want, you can stay for a variety of study groups, prayer circles, craft sessions—ways for folks to engage with each other while pursuing their own spiritual path in a more disciplined way.

One of Thomas's regular practices was to join a group who would gather quietly in meditation, sitting in chairs in a circle around a table laden with unlit candles. A single taper, already lit, stood in the center of the table. As the hour progressed, individuals who felt moved to do so would step to the table and, using the burning taper, light a candle. Then they would name their intention—what they were praying for, what was weighing on their hearts, what they wanted to hold in the light, the reason why they were "lighting one candle against the darkness."

Once, when he was twelve or thirteen years old, Thomas again joined this small gathering of meditators and candle lighters. As the hour neared its end, he suddenly stood and walked quietly to the table. Taking up the taper in the center, he lit a candle and said, "I am lighting this candle for the ambiguity of the world."

The ambiguity: what is good and what only appears to be good; what is true and what only appears to be true. In the trenchant question of E. C. Bentley, quoted in *Places in the Heart,* "Between what matters and what seems to matter, how is the world we know to judge wisely?"

This simple wisdom: that even as we struggle with illness, with death, with catastrophe, we are invited to hold the ambiguity of the world in the light and not to look away. Not to look away from any of it. Perhaps Thomas, who saw this a few years ago as he lit that candle, is teaching us still.

Letter from a friend

Wednesday, July 17

Gary,

For Thomas's birthday, I have asked [two rabbis] to say the Jewish healing prayer in all its fullness at their congregation. (I've been doing the short and adapted version when I come to see Thomas.) It is the holiday of Tisha Bav, which is a holiday of mourning, so they won't be doing the healing prayers until the afternoon. But this is a major thing for them to do on your behalf, so take it as an expression of goodwill and deep hope for Thomas's recovery.

Sending you lots of love.
L P

Friday, July 19

Dear Friends of Thomas:

Thomas had a sixteenth birthday anniversary yesterday unlike any I've ever heard of before. First let me give you an update on him, and then, if you have time, you might want to read the full e-mail about the day's visitors and where we go from here.

This morning, at 8:15, a surgeon came to his room to perform a tracheostomy, cutting a tiny hole in Thomas's windpipe and inserting a plastic device at the front of his neck through which he can breathe on his own (as if receiving the breath of life again as he did on the day he was born). All went well, and the respiratory therapists have been happy with the results. I muttered to one of them that this was a hell of a birthday present for a boy, and David, the therapist, said that, actually, it was a good present under the circumstances: it makes life more comfortable for Thomas and represents a better place than where we were last week.

Tomorrow afternoon, at 2:30, the surgeon will return to Thomas's room to install a "peg"—a tube inserted through the abdomen into the stomach for feeding. The tube that now runs through his nose to his throat and stomach will be removed, and we'll see the boy's face free and clear for the first time in nearly two weeks.

Today visitors had to wear gloves to touch Thomas, masks to be near his face (this made kissing him awkward), and gowns to stay in the room very long, because he has a respiratory staph infection still, and the nurses wanted to protect both visitors and other patients from it.

In the next week or so, we are going to have to make some hard decisions. Depending on how Thomas might respond to care in any of the possible rehab facilities available for someone in his condition, we may be looking at some very harsh realities that will change our lives significantly.

For now, we're not ready to say exactly what those realities might involve. All is too ambiguous and foggy. We have to keep hoping that each day of unconsciousness is a day of rest and regathering of strength, and that soon our boy will begin to show more signs of waking. It's difficult to be hopeful after nearly two weeks of this, but we have no choice. At the same time, we're beginning to have to make plans for contingencies we hope don't come to pass.

As for the birthday, it was sweet and poignant. His first visitors arrived before the tracheostomy and even before visiting hours to deliver balloons and cards.

After the surgery, I was able to spend an hour alone with him, and it reminded me of his first couple of hours of life: he had come into the world by C-section, jaundiced and cold, so the nurses took this tiny infant from his mother, up to the nursery, where they put him on a changing table under a heat lamp. They invited me to rub his back and shoulders and legs and bottom and do what I could to warm him up a little bit and to console him for his rude entry into the world.

On that morning sixteen years ago, I rubbed and patted him and sang him music from *The Magic Flute*. This morning I caressed his head, his arms, his face, and sang him "Happy Birthday." Two mornings of singing to an unconscious boy while worrying about the future. Sixteen full, good years in between. And still counting. I've saved a piece of his birthday cake to serve him on his natal anniversary next year.

Other images of the day:

- After my inability to get a couple of visitors to take the first piece of birthday cake this morning, at last it went to the ninety-five-year-old grandmother of a couple of Thomas's old school chums; she had just celebrated her own birthday a couple weeks ago and was proud to have the first bite of Thomas's cake.

- Eight teenagers gathered around Thomas's bed, all dressed in yellow gowns, masks, and gloves by order of the nurses, and all looking, according to one friend, like something out of *Make Way for Ducklings.*

- Thomas's mother and four of her singing friends lifting glorious harmonies around Thomas's bed.

- Colleagues bringing a basket of fruit to sustain anyone who would eat.

- A nursing technician using the CCU's Polaroid camera to take photos of the guest of honor with a crowd of kids around his bed, then running to get more film because the moment was just too good.

One other image, from Wednesday night, that applies to Thursday. Friends dragged me off to Chastain Park for a wonderful outdoor concert—"Down from the Mountain," an evening of bluegrass music inspired by the Coen brothers' film *O Brother, Where Art Thou*. I'm so grateful to have been there, for the music and for the company.

But I recall especially that at one moment, well after twilight, I looked out over the amphitheater and saw the lighted candles on the tables where people were eating their picnic suppers. The candles flickered, hundreds of tiny flames throughout the expanse of tables and people, the half-lit faces of the crowd turned in rapt attentiveness toward the music that had been our purpose for coming together.

It seems to me that the best thing about Thomas's birthday has been the gathered amphitheater full of people watching over him, from all over the world, and the light shining from your faces into the darkness.

Love and gratitude to all of you from Thomas and his family.

Gary

Letters from friends, Friday, July 19

Gary,

Thank you for sending me the recent update on Thomas.

C.S. Lewis said: "To love at all is to be vulnerable. Love anything and your heart will certainly be wrung and probably be broken. If you want to make sure of keeping it intact, you must give your heart to no one. . . . The only place outside heaven where you can be perfectly safe from all the dangers and perturbations of love is hell."

P C

* * *

Gary,

I was very touched and deeply moved by the news of Thomas's sixteenth birthday. For some reason, it reminded me of my own sixteenth birthday. I had a very dysfunctional childhood and adolescence; my mom died when I was ten and my father was an alcoholic. The summer of my sixteenth year found me living with family friends because my father was on one of his long downward spirals, during which he was unable to take care of his three children and we had to more or less fend for ourselves. My sister, who was living with other friends, organized a surprise sixteenth birthday party for me, and I still have a picture of me blowing out the candles on a cake decorated with a large "16" made out of big gumdrops. Anyway, the point of all of this is that my sister's love made that day special and, quite obviously, memorable to me. Though separated by a thousand or so miles, we remain very, very close today.

What is important in life is love, and clearly the love you and your family have for Thomas, which I am sure was expressed in a thousand ways prior to his illness, will sustain him and all of you throughout this ordeal. And I am sure you know that your colleagues and friends at Emory augment that love with their thoughts and prayers every day.

Thinking of you.
A B

Journal Entry, Saturday, July 20

I'm aware of multiple layers of grief.

First, grieving the at-least-temporary loss of the budding young man—a kind of death of the boy who was (for me a very visible loss, because of my experience early morning of the 8th, when it appeared that he had, in fact, died). Will he ever return?

Second, the grief of perplexity because this state that he is in is not actually death, and it requires us to go on in a way that the punctuation of a funeral would not. This is a kind of limbo that is neither the heaven of life's renewal nor the hell of a burial.

Third, the grief of knowledge that for the foreseeable future our lives must change drastically, though the how of that is unclear to us—whether extended, perhaps interminable nursing care or the finality of his passing. Change, especially profound change, whether welcomed or not, always brings a measure of grief in its train.

We learned yesterday from a social worker friend that the Shepherd Center not only had concluded that they wouldn't be the best rehab option (as they told us yesterday) but also had arrived at a prognosis for Thomas—"persistent vegetative state"—which they had not shared with us. That news is devastating.

Saturday, July 20

Dear Friends of Thomas:

Yesterday afternoon a surgeon inserted a peg into Thomas's stomach. Guiding a tube with a light and a camera on the end down Thomas's upper-GI tract, the surgeon was able to view the inside of the stomach to determine that there are no stress ulcers and no bleeding. He then maneuvered the light toward the upper-left, front quadrant of the stomach, where he wanted to make an incision.

The amazing thing about this procedure is that the surgeon uses the light shining from inside the stomach to guide his cut: when he sees on the camera monitor the spot on the inside of the stomach where he wants the peg, he looks on the outside of the patient's abdomen for the light shining out, and then cuts toward it. There's something powerful about that image—looking for the light shining, impossibly, out of a place where you'd never expect to find it, and then aiming deliberately and incisively toward the light. Look for the light shining out of the darkness and aim for it.

All tubes have been removed from Thomas's nose and mouth, and it's wonderful to see that lovely face we love.

It was also a delight to see Thomas yawn a couple of times on Friday. Who knows what that's all about? He does seem more restful without the tubes in his face, and he may become rested enough to begin waking up.

For now, Thomas seems to be in stable condition, and we're waiting to learn when—probably next week sometime—he might be moved into a facility for acute rehabilitation. I'll let you know more when we know more.

Peace and love to you all.
Gary

Light

"God from God, Light from Light . . ."
—The Nicene Creed

Comatose in ICU, my son
lies mouth agape, a long optical fiber
snaking down his throat into his stomach.
A camera-light, small as a matchhead,

on the fiber's end gives eyes to the surgeon,
who maneuvers the tip
to a spot inside the abdomen.
There, light shines out through the fundal wall,
through muscle and epidermis to the surface—
light from within, out of perpetual darkness,
a glimmering target for the incision
where the feeding tube will enter.
My boy lies still upon the bed.
The surgeon cuts toward the light.

I sit in summer night,
an outdoor amphitheater, brought by friends
for music, a respite from vigil.
I somehow know that Thomas will not recover.
Looking toward the far slope of the half-bowl
I see light from dozens of candles
on concert-goers' picnic tables. Behind each flame,
faces shine, illuminated by the candle glow
like images of saints in gold-leaf icons—
beyond the darkling world, the lambent redeemed.

Onset of winter, days shorten, night deepens.
More difficult the tending of light within—
hearth fire, stove warmth, lamplight dim.
Far back from the highway, across the barren snow fields,

a lone farm stands in the cloud-blacked midnight,
a golden rectangle cast from a farmhouse window,
a single bulb burning high up on the barn.
Tiny sparks amid deep gloom
for anyone looking for light.

Journal Entry, Sunday, July 21

Four doctors today at various times entered and left Thomas's room without once addressing him personally in any fashion. He may as well have been a mannequin. At least two of them did not even touch him while listening to his heart and lungs with a stethoscope. How is that even possible? So far as I'm concerned, they weren't working, not fully. They were not doctoring. They behaved like competent technicians, more like auto mechanics than healers.

Healing in this case is going to take more than applying tools. It's going to require the presence of one human being to another who, despite terrible injury and limitation, is still a living person in his own right and worth being accorded the dignity due to each of us.

Dr. M, whose perfunctory visit lasted all of three minutes, touched someone in the room physically only because I extended my hand to shake his when I introduced myself as Thomas's father. The boy, my boy, on the hospital bed was a case, an object, a thing to study. Goddamn.

Monday, July 22, 11:50 p.m.

Dear Friends of Thomas:

Joseph Campbell says somewhere, "Only at the bottom of the abyss comes the voice of salvation. The darkest moment is the moment when the real message of transformation comes."

This afternoon we didn't hit the bottom, but we certainly slipped over the edge of the abyss before something caught us. It's hard to see what transformation is coming. Hard to believe that any transformation will be for the better.

Shortly after noon, as his mother and I were visiting him, Thomas went into supraventricular tachycardia, his heart racing up to 193 beats a minute and his blood pressure going haywire for nearly three-quarters of an hour. He had been off the ventilator since 2 p.m. Saturday, breathing on his own, his heart beating regularly in the fifties and sixties. He had looked to be doing a pretty good job of becoming a candidate for acute rehab, which requires that he be off the ventilator for at least 48 hours before admission. He was at 46 hours when this happened. Why it happened is not clear to the medical team. It may be that breathing for so long on his own strength wore him out.

The upshot of it was a dire emergency. A team of nurses and technicians and respiratory therapists and, eventually, a couple of MDs worked for about an hour to get his heart under control and his blood pressure down. The nurse in charge behaved with absolutely masterful professional focus that was inspiring to witness—a combination of competence and love that fills me with awe. At the end of it all, though, she could not hold back tears as she broke down from the strain and from the near futility of it all.

Thomas was stable enough by 1:15 that his mother and I left to look into a rehab center that could possibly take him for the long term. About an hour later, the hospital reached us to call us back, saying Thomas had "taken a turn for the worse." After what we had witnessed earlier, we expected the very worst.

When we got to his room, the nurse told us he was no longer breathing on his own; the ventilator was doing all the work. His pupils were fixed. He appeared to be gone. But over the next hour or so, his strong heart kept beating, and in time he began breathing on his own, with a little push on each breath from the ventilator. When I left him this evening around 8:30 we seemed to be back to square one—the place of anguish, uncertainty, a feeling of doom, a need for hope.

It's just over two weeks since Thomas suffered his cardiac arrest and was taken to the emergency room. As Alexis and I were leaving home that night to follow the ambulance to the hospital, I thought it important to call someone to meet us there and help us hold our emotions together or, if we couldn't do that, at least find the pieces again after they shattered.

I telephoned Susan Henry-Crowe, the university chaplain and dean of the chapel at Emory, who has been not only a pastor to me (and to many of us in the community) for many years but also a dear and close friend of my family. Susan met us at the emergency room, and as we waited for a nurse or doctor to come tell us what was going on, what Thomas's condition was—whether he was even still alive—she prayed with us a prayer that I will never forget.

Alluding to Jesus's anguish in Gethsemane the night before his crucifixion, and the terrible darkness following his death, Susan prayed, "Oh, God, you know the agony of this night. . . ."

And yes, I thought—the gospels tell of the agony of that night when Jesus prayed for the cup of suffering to be taken from him, and when the Father, God, in whom he trusted witnessed the helplessness of his son at the hands of those who "know not what they do." Perhaps the agony of that night was similar to what we felt in that waiting room. It was the agony of seeing how fragile and vulnerable a human life truly is.

I do believe God knows the anguish of such nights, the agony of our night, which has now become a little more than a fortnight—not much longer than the Wimbledon tennis tournament by the calendar, but unbelievably long when measured on the emotional clock. I can hardly remember when it began.

I do not know what God will do to redeem this time—to bring good out of it—but I continue to hold to the hope that good will come. Whether it is Thomas's waking and his return to us or, more likely, something else, perhaps quiet and surprising and incomprehensible, something good must come.

Always in these circumstances it seems easy to see coincidences. One coincidence I've thought of many times over the past two weeks is the aptness (in retrospect) of the Old Testament lesson read at the last church service Thomas and I attended together.

It was the week before his cardiac arrest. That Sunday, the service was a special one to note the conclusion of Vacation Bible School at the Episcopal Church of the Epiphany, where we are members. Thomas had spent the previous week volunteering to help lead the young children through activities. One of the things he has always liked is looking after younger kids, and he had sometimes thought of being a teacher (when he wasn't thinking of being either a professional wrestling announcer, a psychiatrist, or a chef). That week he also worked in the kitchen helping to prepare lunch every day for the kids and teachers. One of the teachers later remarked to me how gracefully and matter-of-factly Thomas took charge of the salad making. So however much he usually resisted going to Sunday morning worship services, he was genuinely interested in being at this one. It was the culmination of something he had felt proud and happy to be part of.

The lesson for that morning was one of the hardest stories in the Bible, and one that has perplexed me forever.

As I sat beside my son, we heard the story of God's commanding Abraham to take his only and long-awaited and well-loved son, Isaac, up to the mountain to sacrifice him. This seems to me to be a story about God as a bizarre and capricious tyrant at best or, at worst, sadistically cruel.

I've always thought that Abraham was wrong not to refuse, not to say no to God—or not to offer to lay himself on the altar in Isaac's place, as any father would lay himself down or any mother herself in place of their daughter or son. And yet—however much I might think of myself as ready to lay myself on the altar in place of my son, I also recall how many times I have chafed at the inconvenience of having a child who was not "easy," whose illness complicated our lives. My guilt runneth over.

We're not told what Abraham was thinking on that day—only that he went through what God and life had put before him. This is what Abraham was given to do, and with whatever emotion was in his heart, he moved on through it, understanding that his life—and Isaac's—were beyond his control.

In the end, the sacrifice became unnecessary, and God provided a ram as a substitute for the altar, prompting Abraham to name the place "God provides."

To be honest, I don't see any rams in the thicket at this point. Though I am told to believe in miracles, I am not confident that there will be a sudden and unexpected resolution that will make everything right and return us to life as it was before. But I do believe that God will provide a way through this terrible time, somehow. And we—and Thomas—will be transformed by love and faith and hope.

One of the hymns for that last Sunday when Thomas and I worshipped together was "Be Not Afraid," a song that had been a theme for the Vacation Bible School. Thomas did not often sing around the house, and he rarely sang hymns in church. But I recall the smile on his face as I stood next to him and heard him belting out the words by heart: "Be not afraid. I go before you always. Come, follow me, and I will give you rest."

I have wondered whether Thomas has heeded that phrase, "be not afraid," and is going on. He seems to me to be taking leave from us slowly to give us time to touch him and grieve over his departure while still in his presence.

Under the mercy of God,
Gary

Letters from friends, Monday, July 22

Dear Gary,

My heart goes out to you tonight.

I never hear the story of Abraham and Isaac without remembering how deeply I was changed by Kierkegaard's exploration of the story in his book Fear and Trembling. *Now that I am a parent, the story is more torturous and mysterious. It's odd—I hadn't read the book since college and recently bought myself a new copy.*

Tonight, I went with some friends to see Anna Deavere Smith at Woodruff Arts Center, an event of the National Black Arts Festival. Her art is really journalism in its purest form—she bears witness, she seeks and finds truth, and then mirrors it for the rest of us to see and contemplate. Her artistry is in her ability to see and hear many different truths at once, internalize them all and project them out again in a form powerful yet loving enough to draw us into realities we might rather ignore.

As I watched her, I found myself thinking of Thomas and his openness to truths. And I thought of you, his family, and how cloudy the view must be from where you are—how precarious you must feel. It is OK to be there for a while, to move slowly, to savor your love of Thomas and to give Alexis the love and care she needs now as you move through these foggy truths together. You have two wonderful children who deserve all the love, care, and respect you can show them. Our children need to see our fragility as well as our strengths, you know; not only is it honest—a truth—but it also shows them respect, trust.

Do not ever hesitate to let us know how we can help. You are in our thoughts and prayers. Even as Thomas has slept these past weeks, he has deeply changed and opened the hearts of many people. He still has gifts to give.

S S

Dear Gary,

I received your note, and I can hear your voice in it. I don't know if the human psyche is built for this kind of suffering.

Until the past fifty years, people who were extremely ill did not tarry. There was no hope. Now we have hope, but the roller-coaster ride is so very, very terribly taxing.

I am stopping to pray and then praying with every task I do. This I learned when I was a Catholic child. I'm no longer Catholic, but the meditation has stuck with me. I am speaking to God, to Thomas, to his nurses and doctors, to you, Kate, and Alexis.

Much love.
P C

Journal Entry, Wednesday, July 24

Maybe every disaster, every heartbreak, even possibly every death, can be chalked up to an imperfection of love. Had I, for instance, loved Thomas perfectly, or even better, I would have taken him with me to the retreat that weekend before this happened; would therefore have had him more near to my attention; would therefore have listened to what was going on in him; would therefore have done what I could to prevent all this from happening.

Or coming home and finding him as he was, would have ignored all the dirty clothes on the floor, the soup he'd left untended on the stove burner (which was still on), the impatience I felt rising in me because of his illness. Would not have said or done whatever it was that prompted him to say, at one point early in the evening, "Dad, if you aren't going to be nice, just leave."

Fatigue; self-centeredness; the distraction of returning from out of town; the desire to attend to my hunger, to read a book, to go to bed early in anticipation of a busy week—all these things made me less than perfectly attentive to what Thomas was experiencing and needing. To be able to attend perfectly to everyone in our lives every moment—this would be to have a knowledge and energy beyond any human power I've ever witnessed, though God knows I've seen men and women who do it better than I.

Reading Kierkegaard's meditation on Abraham and Isaac in *Fear and Trembling* yesterday, I came to the passage where he contrasts fathers who have lost their beloved sons because of an act of God, on one hand (sickness, storm, avalanche, flood), to Abraham, on the other, whose faith prepared him to act to cause his own son's death. On Monday, when Thomas appeared to have left us after his tachycardia emergency, it felt as if all this struggle and anguish had, blessedly, been taken out of our hands by him and by God. His passing would now be not the result of a decision we would have to make, not something we would actively initiate through doctor's orders and the removal of all that supports his life. It would be an act of God. Today I find myself wondering whether, in time, his mother and I will find decision and action placed back in our hands, finally our responsibility.

A quotation from the film *Road to Perdition*, a line spoken by Paul Newman about his character's son: "Sons are put on earth to trouble their fathers."

I suppose I'd add that it's not because they necessarily want to.

Journal Entry, Thursday, July 25

Thomas seems to be gone in a way that he was not before the tachycardia on Monday. After the EMTs resuscitated him following the first cardiac arrest at home, I had a sense of the boy still there, unresponsive perhaps but there, maybe hearing and understanding all the love being expressed around him. Now, it is as if, having borne the intrusions and humiliations of the CCU for two weeks, he had finally had enough. The medical team that kept his body alive on Monday worked mightily to prevent another cardiac arrest, but it feels like despite their efforts he has decided to take his leave from his fleshy home. Enough, he says.

Friday, July 26

Dear Friends of Thomas:

Some of you have wondered about the hiatus in updates on Thomas since Monday night. This week his mother and I have been traveling in a fog, through terrain where we were never certain to find solid footing, and it seemed, in a way, pointless to tell you what path we were on when we might find ourselves within an hour on a different one.

We started the week anticipating Thomas's move to a rehabilitation program, then found ourselves grieving his apparent sudden death and signing a do-not-resuscitate order as he went back on the ventilator, then watched him begin to breathe on his own again and fight through infection and high fevers, to the point that he is now resting peacefully, pink-cheeked, off the ventilator once more, and seeming like a sleeping cherub. It has never been more clear that we and the medical staff are not in control of this situation.

After Thomas's tachycardia and later respiratory arrest Monday afternoon, his neurologist ordered another EEG. He said that each of the four EEGs performed since Thomas's admission showed further decline in brain activity.

This evening we met with a pediatric neurologist from Emory—a woman who proved to be an excellent teacher of laypeople like us about the extraordinary complexities of brain injury. She showed us images of the CT scan she had ordered today and compared them to the images of the CT scan the day Thomas was admitted to the hospital. Today's scan showed tissue loss in the front and sides of the brain, permanent damage to the basal ganglia, and atrophy around the ventricles as well as other global damage.

All of this amounts to saying that Thomas as we knew him will never reappear in this life. The damage to the areas of the brain that control memory, motor skills, and language is simply too great, and irreversible. And in all likelihood another event like Monday's tachycardia would damage the brain still more.

Over the course of five days this week we have had long, painful, and searching conversations with doctors, nurses, social workers, chaplains, and hospice workers, as well as with many of you, our close and dear friends. It has become increasingly clear that, while we do not give up hope for a miracle, we must begin to ask ourselves what's in the best interest of Thomas at this point. What would Thomas want in these circumstances? Ultimately, of course, this question is impossible for any of us to answer. But if we can respond from what we have come to know about Thomas during his sixteen years with us so far, we believe he would be loath to continue in a state of nearly complete unresponsiveness, inability to communicate, total dependence on others for the most basic needs of feeding and hygiene, and continuing vulnerability to infections, fevers, and eventually organ failure. For many of these reasons, he has always hated even the very fact of his having Addison's disease. He once remarked about a year ago that he expected that the illness "will get me in the end." He said this with his customary ironic knowingness, as if in jest. But like all humor, it had a serious basis. He surely could not have anticipated or wanted to be in the condition he is in.

So we are looking at transferring Thomas to hospice care, where he would be kept comfortable, stimulated through music, movement, and talk, and able to be visited by the host of family and friends who have made their way to the critical care unit since July 8. The DNR would be in effect, and if he showed signs of improvement in the weeks to come, he could be moved to rehab. More likely, he will go from us like a young tree in a long drought.

I know my eyes see through the lens of fatherhood, but he seems to me the loveliest young man, like a sleeping prince. One of you remarked this week that, lying there with his eyes closed and a glow to his cheeks, he looked like the sunset seen from Key West—resplendent, beautiful, and mysterious. As his father, I want you to know him in this way.

Of course, it's not all peace and beauty. It's also incomprehensible, grotesquely unfair, and cause for rage and wild tears, then numbness. I do not know what's sustaining his family through this time other than the love and friendship of you, and the love and mercy of God, for all of which I give thanks.

Blessings to you.
Gary

Journal Entry, Saturday, July 27

What keeps us going in the face of all we are dealing with is not courage but the inevitable daily rising of the sun and the need to greet it each day and move into it. If it weren't for that regularity, I'm not certain how I'd get into the demands of the morning. At the same time, the routine feels intolerably painful. I don't know how I can stand another visit to this hospital—coming into the parking deck, taking the ticket from the clock gate, driving up the ramp to the third level and looking for a space, coming through the door to the pedestrian bridge between the deck and the hospital, through the door to the ICU/CCU, past the two waiting rooms with their televisions playing to different audiences or to no one. It's insufferable. But I don't know how I will be able to stand having no reason to come here, an end to my purpose in making the daily visits. I've reached the point of prayer at which I don't know what to ask for.

Journal Entry, Thursday, August 1

Great anger welling up in me, all of it directed at people who seem indifferent, callous, unhelpful. All of it, though, I'm sure, has its source in the impossible place where we find ourselves. A couple of friends want us to "give Thomas every chance; the brain has a miraculous way to heal itself"—as if we haven't been trying to give him every chance, or as if the doctors and nurses have not read the writing on the wall for weeks about the direction this is going, the way this particular brain is not going to heal itself.

Then there is the reminder from a friend that Scott Peck begins *The Road Less Traveled* with the sentence, "Life is difficult," followed by the suggestion that once we accept this truth, life becomes less difficult. I suppose there is what Howard Nemerov calls "some mean-spirited moral point in that"—some encouragement to find the lesson in a miserable situation. This reminder comes from someone who lives in a million-dollar house, has a country club membership (its own form of life challenge, I suppose), and recently returned from vacation in Europe. What truth am I supposed to accept from that difficulty?

Meeting today with Dr. W., who wrote orders for hospice care. Later a nurse withdrew Thomas's feeding tube—no more nourishment going in. The beginning of a horrible process of slow starvation. I feel oddly removed emotionally from this process—as if I cried all my tears in the first three weeks and have run dry; or as if, once the decision for hospice has been made, all has become clinical and detached, the way a father-to-be learns the Lamaze method and coaches the mother through labor, helping as best he can but using technique to distance himself from the pain and struggle of the moment.

Journal Entry, Friday, August 2

People usually refer to this experience of losing a child as "every parent's nightmare." It's clear that, from the moment our children are born, we are aware of "the Undertoad," as John Irving's Garp refers to it—the thing in the world that has the potential to snatch our children from us before we're ready to let go. Wendell Berry captures the anxiety, the worry brought by the uncertainty of the future.

To My Children, Fearing for Them
by Wendell Berry

Terrors are to come. The earth
is poisoned with narrow lives.
I think of you. What you will

live through, or perish by, eats
at my heart. What have I done? I
need better answers than there are

to the pain of coming to see
what was done in blindness,
loving what I cannot save. Nor,

your eyes turning toward me,
can I wish your lives unmade
though the pain of them is on me.

"Terrors are to come." Terror came in the form of a honeybee when Thomas was two. We were picnicking at a park—his mother, sister, he, and I—when the little redheaded boy reached in curiosity to the thing moving nearby on the grass. Before we knew what was happening, he had wrapped his small hand around the beautifully striped insect, which reciprocated by stinging him. His immediate cry of pain—prolonged, loud, and racking his body—launched us all into panicked motion. What if he was allergic to the sting and suffered anaphylactic shock? We didn't know what his reaction might be. And we were miles from medical help. Fortunately, by the time we'd gathered all our things and hurried to our car, he was calming down and clearly was not in danger. But our terror had been real.

All of this that has happened over the past four weeks—at least the seemingly inevitable outcome of it—has carried little surprise once the initial crisis of the cardiac arrest was past. What has eaten at my soul is the frequency with which we've had to confront questions whose answers—urgent, irreversible, impossible—would either hasten or delay the outcome. Should we take path A or path B? What about treatment C or treatment D? Let's do this—no, wait, we can't because of that. There is the sense that, yes, this situation is largely out of my control but also, regrettably, still very much in my hands through conversations with doctors, nurses, Kate, Alexis, and maybe, in some way, even Thomas himself. Input I'd rather not have to give, thought I'd rather not have to think—my unwillingness to weigh in on ultimate matters may be a symptom of my general passivity in the face of life but also a legitimate response to what feels overwhelming. The pain of it is on me.

Friday, August 2

Dear Friends of Thomas:

Tomorrow morning, Thomas will be moved from the hospital, his home for the past month, to Hospice Atlanta, where we will begin to help him along in the last stage of his journey in this life.

We have not arrived at this moment with anything but grief and heartbreak. We are in a fearful place, on holy ground. But we do believe that this is the best way, now, to care for and love Thomas—to let him go fully where he has already gone. His physicians have given us no reason to hope that he will recover, and in the meantime his systems are beginning to fail because of neurological damage.

We don't know at this point how much longer we will have him, but we encourage you to visit him if you want to and can.

Not all is dark clouds and despair: we have been upheld in these past weeks by sharing with you the stories about Thomas that we and you have come to cherish during the years he has been with us. This is an opportunity for us to celebrate the beneficence and joy this young man has brought to us, while we still have him among us.

Gary

Journal Entry, Saturday, August 3

We moved Thomas today from DeKalb Medical Center to Hospice Atlanta. I was consumed by a great feeling of dread all morning—maybe what I would feel if I were a prisoner being moved to death row: the weight of waiting, and of waiting for a thing you would rather not have happen, in fact a thing that you would give almost anything to have come no closer.

Unbearable weight of responsibility—the weight of guilt for surviving, the weight of guilt for not having avoided all this and made it unnecessary, the weight of duty for seeing that every step along the rest of the way is perfectly fitting and ultimately helpful.

The black-and-white photos of Thomas taken by Emory photographer Ann Watson (just a month before his cardiac arrest, as it happened) are taped to the wall over his bed. Somehow, they serve his spirit and memory better than a video loop could do. In their stillness, the energy and light from within him look potential rather than kinetic, ready to burst out of the bind of their two dimensions and their colorless world with power and brilliance.

Incredible dullness of grief takes hold, almost as a way to protect myself, almost as though experiencing the world fully would expose all nerve endings to the reality of all the pain that has ever been.

Monday, August 5

Dear Friends of Thomas:

This morning I got to the hospice around 7:15, grateful to have time alone with Thomas—a good three hours, during which I read Psalms to the unconscious young man, prayed aloud with him, recited poetry, sang to him, and regaled him with reminiscences of our first trip to New Orleans together two years ago, a belated Christmas present delayed to the early summer because he had become ill when we first planned to go. It was a city that appealed to his imagination before he ever saw it, especially because of the food to be had there (he loved Cajun dishes). He laughed wide-eyed on our carriage ride through the French Quarter when the driver remarked, as we turned onto Bourbon Street, that here was a place "where boys will be boys—and where boys will be girls." We munched beignets at Café du Monde, had dinner on a riverboat while listening to jazz, and took in the music at Preservation Hall. We traveled to the city and back via Amtrak, which gave us the luxury of a nine-hour game of five-hundred rummy on the way home (interrupted by lunch, dinner, and visits to the club car). The running score reached something like 5,820 to 5,660. I'm not certain who won.

After more than fourteen hours at the hospice today with Thomas and friends, I'm sitting at home now listening to Bach organ toccatas and fugues at full blast. This seems the only viable alternative to throwing dinner plates off my apartment balcony into the parking lot.

The surreality of the past month can have been surpassed only by the experience of the disciples after Good Friday, I suppose. How did all of this happen, they must have asked. There we were, hanging out and passing the days in good purpose with a loving fellow who was teaching us profound things, and then—boom, catastrophe.

I am still waiting for Easter and wonder what it will look like. I believe in it, but my eyes are weary from weeping and can't focus yet on seeing. There's still the tomb to be endured.

Many of you who have visited Thomas at Hospice Atlanta have commented on the surprising loveliness of the place. Indeed, it is lovely—gentle and peaceful and good. Yet there is something terrible about its beauty—a wonderful place for me to pass my last days if I'm a hundred and twenty, but not for my son at sixteen. How amazing that such a tranquil spot can be the scene of such a nightmare—sort of a paradigm for our existence on what the Book of Common Prayer calls "this fragile earth, our island home." Here on this planet the manifold delights of life compete with child murder, rape, bombs, and the likes of lupus and Lou Gehrig's disease. And Addison's disease.

I don't know what we are to make of all this, except that I am confident that some good will come of it, and that meanwhile we have to find some way to be for each other as you have been for Thomas and his family. I don't know how I can ever repay any of you for what you have given us over the past four weeks. But I will always try to be present for you as you have been present for us.

Peace and blessings to you.

Gary

Journal Entry, Monday, August 5

The drama of Thomas's dark passage, like the drama, in miniature, of every holy story—for me, as a Christian, the drama of Abraham and Isaac but also the drama of the agony in the Garden, the uncertainty of waiting, the death of an innocent, the hope that even out of the most severe catastrophe God can create good—that out of this formless chaos can come a world of light and beauty. Can I even believe that?

Where is Thomas's spirit? No longer in the body. His body has been for him such a fallible instrument by which to manifest his spirit in this world, though that body continues to go on despite all. But clearly he is somewhere still here, maybe most fully in the sweetness of certain gatherings of friends and family members. His spirit gathers us and somehow holds and nurtures us.

Journal Entry, Tuesday, August 6

Talking with a friend this evening, I remarked that Thomas's premature death, at sixteen, may be a blessing for him as well as a tragic loss. Tragically, he will miss the joys of sex, marriage, and having children. Blessedly, on the other hand, he will miss all the sorrows and travails that come with adulthood. To which she said, "Like sex, marriage, and having children?" It's a humorous toss-off line but one that has some truth.

Journal Entry, Wednesday, August 7

Clergy! God, spare me! I know they mean well, and some are genuine bearers of grace and light. And some are people I love dearly and admire deeply. Some are heroes and heroines. But . . .

A part-time chaplain came by the hospice room today. He couldn't get my name straight after three tries. He had stopped in even after being told by the nurse, in our behalf, that we didn't need or want a visit. He came and chatted in his unhelpful, generic, and cheery way, then summoned us to the bedside for prayer. There were about eight of us in the room, and compelled, I suppose, by our own sense of what was gracious under the circumstances, we dutifully assumed hand-holding positions around the bed; he then said he'd like to start with a song—the first verse of "Have Thine Own Way, Lord," which he sang before praying. No one else joined in singing. I could have screamed through the entire prayer.

Then this afternoon another pastor, this one a friend, likewise couldn't just say goodbye and leave after visiting. Without asking the other people in the room, he said, before leaving, "Let's pray." End of conversation. Again, holding hands around the bed.

Do I think my prayers are better than theirs? I don't believe so—any more than I believe that their prayers are superfluous. Their prayers matter for many reasons. I just want quiet.

Another clergyman, a trustee of Emory, came by after a hurried conversation with a female colleague at my office at the university. He misunderstood what she was saying and thought that some relative of *hers* was here at the hospice, ill and dying. In his usual busy-ness he had not bothered to listen to the full story, had failed to learn that it was *my* son who was dying, not a relative of my colleague's. Nevertheless, conscientious and dutiful, he had come to Hospice Atlanta for a pastoral visit. He came into the room, and I don't know whether he was surprised to see me there, since he likely would have expected the family of my colleague to be present. But he said, "I'm so sorry to hear the news from Mary Ann. Now—what is Thomas's relationship to her, exactly?"

The word "dunderhead" came to mind. Similarly, the word "ass." He was startled, of course, when I had to correct him by saying that Thomas was my son, no relation to my colleague. Then he insisted on knowing all about Addison's disease, and this meant starting at the beginning, picking up the story from five or six weeks ago.

It has made me think that there needs to be a rack outside the room, with several stacks of information sheets: take sheet A if your last visit was within twenty-four hours, sheet B if more than three days ago, sheet C if more than a week, sheet D if more than three weeks, and sheet F if this is your first visit. And if you don't know whom you're visiting, go ahead and leave now.

It's not just clergy. Other well-meaning people say exactly the wrong thing. Stepping into a coffee shop near the campus, I saw a professor I know who was seated at a table. As I passed and said hello, he stopped me and said, "I hear your son is in hospice." Yes, I said, and thanked him for caring. "Well," he said as I prepared to leave, "chin up." What? Chin up? It's like saying have a nice day despite the apocalypse.

Journal Entry, Friday, August 9

This terrible waiting is like being in labor, but with a far less joyful outcome in view (can I have faith that there will be joy for Thomas?). Both in the waiting for death and in the waiting for birth there is the same dread of what we will have to go through—the pain of coming into a new and unknown life.

I sometimes wonder whether Thomas feared the future or was simply and more healthily content in the present. Once, when he was fourteen or fifteen, as we sat at the dining room table before clearing away the dishes after dinner, he said to me, "Dad, I think I want to live here forever." I smiled and asked what he meant. In this place? Was he going to continue living in this particular apartment or in our apartment complex, or what exactly did he have in mind? No, he said—"I want to always live with you." I laughed and said, "Well, we'll see what you think about that in a few years."

Of course I felt gratitude for the father-son bond that his comment suggested, and the satisfaction that he seemed to find in the kind of domestic arrangement we'd arrived at despite some rugged terrain and hairpin detours along the way. He was at an age when he did not yet need to think about venturing across the seas and traversing the Himalayas on his own. That would come, though it would take some stretching on his part.

For instance, Thomas hated going to camp, because he always got homesick. After our first trip to New Orleans, a friend of his mentioned that he was going to a weeklong archery camp in the North Georgia woods, where the campers would be sleeping in tents and doing their business in the brush among the trees. Would Thomas like to come along? Thomas thought he would, and so we made all the preparations for his roughing it in a tent—buying a sleeping bag and ground cover, waterproof jacket, good boots, and so on. I dropped him off in the middle of a forest at the end of a dirt road and headed home.

Next day the camp director called from a farmhouse to which he had driven Thomas and said Thomas wanted to come home. He put Thomas on the phone. Thomas pleaded with me. He begged. He cried. He twisted every heartstring. So at first I caved in and agreed to pick him up the next day. But after consulting with friends and my conscience and whatever parental instincts I had, I decided that it would be best for him to stick it out. When he met me at the dirt road the next day, expecting to go home, he was furious and felt abandoned when I told him that he would have to stay, and that I was going to go home by myself. At the end of the week, when the camp was finally over, I drove up to the woods for the third time and loaded his gear and him into the car. For the first twenty minutes of our ride he maintained an impregnable silence. When I suggested we stop for some burgers and milkshakes he began to let his cold hatred of me melt. By the time we had eaten and gotten onto the interstate, he was regaling me with stories of the camp, which he felt proud to have completed, though he never got used to bowel movements in the brush. He even shared with me the secret Indian name that the camp director had conferred on him. He swore me to secrecy, and I said of course. We were okay again.

This feels like he's going away to camp forever, and I'm the one who will be homesick.

Journal Entry, Sunday, August 11

My first child, Alexis, is having as hard a time as anyone. She is about to lose her only sibling, with whom she has had a close and loving bond since he was born. They have leaned on each other through their parents' divorce, through multiple moves, through their own respective illnesses and challenges—even through the usual sibling spats and donnybrooks.

Yesterday, as she prepares to begin her first year of college at Emory, she and I went to a reception and information session for new students starting school in a couple of weeks. We arrived late for what I thought would be just a meet-and-greet, but which turned out to be students in one room for Q&A with college administrators, and parents in another. I experienced a great sense of dissociation—of inability to fit the conversations going on around me with what I had left in the hospice across town. On one hand, dorm etiquette and club opportunities; on the other hand, thoughts about a memorial service and burial.

It's hard to see how we are going to manage both of these transitions emotionally—Alexis going to college, and Thomas going off to somewhere. It will be very tough for her—the intensity of meeting new people and becoming immersed in a new life while the old life is still hauntingly passing away. How in the world is she going to get through this? How will any of us?

I talked yesterday with a friend about the question that perplexes me: where is Thomas's spirit as he lies in this deep coma. Not to be too mystical or sentimental about it, but I think his spirit does meet us in some way whenever and wherever he is loved. Where we tell stories about him, memories in common, shared grief and shared laughter, we evoke (or invoke?) his personality and vitality. In that sense, his spirit has gone beyond the inadequate instrument of his original body and into the still-vibrant body of the community around him.

Maybe this is how the love of Jesus for everyone he encountered went into the body of the early church, his followers—through the sharing of stories about him, through the mutual embrace of the community members, through the urge to live up to the full humanity of what they had witnessed.

Journal Entry, Wednesday, August 14

Each bite of each meal I eat feels like a small betrayal of the son who has received no food now for almost two weeks. The only reason for my eating is that, while he is now served best by having no nutrition, I am supposed (according to all rational counsel from friends) to maintain my own health and strength. I need to continue being present for him, for Alexis, for others.

There are so many feeding stories in the Bible—Elijah and the ravens; manna in the desert; Jesus and the five thousand; the meal on the road to Emmaus. There are also fasting stories, though oddly not so many. The Son of Man you will not always have with you, so eat and celebrate life while he is here. My son will not always be with us—but can I not fast with him while he is fasting?

In the end, Thomas's body failed him. We can say, as I have heard others say and have said myself in the past six weeks, "I failed him." If only, if only, if only—if only he had had a different body. But he had the one he had, and it—and we—failed him in countless ways large and small. Just as we fail each other every day.

But the sign and wonder I've seen in Thomas's long work of dying is the gathering of people determined, in the end, not to fail him or each other. He has called us to a greater love of each other. And in that regard, he seems to me a small reflection of the One with whose meaning and identity he sometimes wrestled—as all of us in various ways have wrestled, more or less.

Thursday, August 15

Dear Friends of Thomas:

Some of you have written to ask about Thomas's status, and I write only to let you know that he is still, barely, with us at this hour. He is breathing gently, with a weak pulse and very low blood pressure. His body, which seemed to him to falter so often in the past few years and to be such a feeble vessel for his spirit, has turned out to have a strong, strong heart. But he is wearing out. We are grateful for your continuing prayers for him and for us.

Journal Entry, Friday, August 16

Gray skies after the night's fierce storms. Thomas looks, in Kate's words, like a hungry baby bird—his head back on his pillow, his mouth open, as if avid for the food he is not receiving. His bones look fragile as dry pine twigs under his hospital gown.

I think of what it must mean to Kate to see her son dying, as Mary watched her son die—unfairly, with agonizing slowness, leaving the structure of the universe dismantled and in chaos. I think of other fathers whose sons found death (or whose sons death found) before their fathers—Shakespeare, J. S. Bach, Lincoln, Leland Stanford, Mark Twain, W. E. B. DuBois, Robert Frost, the untold millions whose sons never returned from war, sons murdered by mobs, John Keats's father, Joseph Kennedy, anonymous coal miners, fathers of accident victims, fathers of children dead of plague and influenza and malaria. My own father and mother, who lost their second daughter at the age of twenty-five to an accident caused by a drunken driver (as I lost a sister).

What we mourning fathers share is the loss of hope for certain things—for the pride of seeing our own flourishing vitality continued in the lives of our sons; for the unique camaraderie that can grow from this singular, father-son relationship (in a way, a kind of mentoring of oneself through a sort of second chance that sees in the son the possible fruition of one's unattained promise); for the reminders of one's own boyhood and youth. (It was delightful to see Thomas working on his plans for a restaurant that would be laid out like a map of the world, with food from different cultures being served in their respective parts of the map. What might he have achieved in another ten or twenty years, after culinary school perhaps?)

Journal Entry, Saturday, August 17

I'm angry enough at the universe that I could spit rocks through windows. It is time for this absurdity, this drawn-out passage to death, to end. What is the point? What lesson are we to learn from continuing this vigil further? Patience? Trust? How to go on loving and caring for Thomas when he himself is no longer capable? The organism that carried him, his body, is simply going on and on with all its functions and proving not only that we do not live by bread alone, but also that we don't even need the bread beyond a certain level.

The umbilical cord had to be cut in order for Thomas and his mother both to live after his birth. The feeding tube had to be removed for Thomas to find the way into another manner of living. But what horrors life confronts us with. Not all the good, rational arguments for removing the tube can diminish the sense of appalling unfairness a parent feels at being given the task of choosing, for their child, either a life of unconscious vegetation or a three-week regimen of starvation leading to death.

I have heard, these weeks, the phrase "at the mercy of"—as in, "We are at the mercy of any infection or contingency that might come along." We are all, of course, always "at the mercy of" whatever it is that will carry us out of life. But this does not feel like mercy. There must be a word for this way of talking about something by illustrating its opposite. We are at God's mercy, but this long-drawn-out ordeal feels like anything other than mercy.

* * *

What would Thomas's obituary say of him?

That he loved professional wrestling but was, himself, a gentle soul who had difficulty killing bugs.

That he laughed at *Friends, Seinfeld, The Simpsons* but also found *The Sopranos* engrossing.

That his keen intelligence took note of and found humor in the curiosities and inconsistencies and absurdities of human existence, but had little patience for chemistry, algebra, or foreign languages.

That, at fourteen, he met a girl named Zoe in a martial arts class and was smitten, to the point of telling her, "Zoe means life, and you mean life to me." They had a movie date once, with me as driver, but she lived an hour away, and the relationship fizzled when the martial arts class ended.

That he was drawn to women and charmed them, as he did an Emory undergraduate we encountered at the Atlanta airport when we learned we would be on the same flight to Baltimore. She and I had served on a committee together and recognized each other at the boarding gate, so when she said hi, I introduced her and Thomas. We chatted for a bit, and then she took a seat in the gate area several seats away from where he and I had been sitting. Thomas was soon up and sitting beside her, and they talked animatedly until we boarded. I have no idea what they were talking about.

That he had a hundred-pound heavy bag in his bedroom and regularly boxed it in his boxer undershorts. He weighed not much more than the bag.

That he sang a good falsetto along with the Bee Gees in "Staying Alive."

That he was learning to play the blues on an Alvarez acoustic guitar that I bought him for his twelfth birthday, though he hankered to go electric.

That he was an aspiring chef who found himself a job as a busboy at the local sandwich shop, Urban Cannibals, because he liked hanging out there on the way home from school and chatting up the two cool dudes, Steve and Richard, who managed the place and put together the sandwiches. (Steve and Richard came to his memorial service, bawling their eyes out as they spoke to me at the reception afterward.)

That he experimented with variations of hairstyles ranging from blue mohawk to bleached crew cut to Beatles mop-top to shaved head.

That he was growing into a thoughtful and caring mentor for younger children and might have made a great teacher or coach. In his last winter, it snowed while we were visiting my parents in Pennsylvania, and he delighted in romping through the backyard with his younger cousins, showing them how to make snowballs and getting hit with a few himself.

That he had been baptized by a Lutheran minister, raised by a Congregationalist minister, attended a Baptist church most of his life and, lately, an Episcopal church, but tended to think of himself as a Buddhist. Once, as he was busing tables at Urban Cannibals, someone took note of his shaved head (it was during that phase) and asked if he were a skinhead. No, he said—I'm a Buddhist.

Wednesday, August 21, 2002

Dear Friends:

At 12:08 this morning, Thomas departed this life peacefully, quietly, with the simple slowing and, finally, cessation of his breathing. He appeared comfortable and untroubled to the end. Next to his bed, among many touchstones and reminders of his life, stood a card that a friend had sent last week, showing an icon of Mary bending over the dead Jesus, with the text from the Orthodox Christian liturgy: "My son, my senses are wounded and my heart is burned, as I see you dead. Yet, trusting in your resurrection, I magnify you."

We rejoice in the love and blessing God has brought to us through Thomas. We give thanks that he has been part of our family and our communities for sixteen years. And we look forward to the play of his spirit among you and us for years to come, as well as to the promise of his new life in God's mercy. May light perpetual shine upon Thomas. And may we share in the peace and comfort he has found at last.

Sending you peace and love,
Gary

Holy Saturday

Journal Entry, August 22, 2002

Guilt and self-hatred are the temptations: how can I not weep continuously since his death yesterday morning? Weep for the loss of him but also for the loss of something in me.

God, let me know fully the depth of this grief—let me feel the utter abyss of it, let me experience all the nightmare misery of it. Let me express in whatever despairing half-sentences and groaning inarticulate phrases the complete hopelessness of it.

But bring me back from it also. Help me not to waste this pain.

Journal Entry, September 2

The question continues to gnaw at me: what if the hope that Thomas now is at rest, at peace, is really only an empty hope? What if, rather, those last hours on the evening of July 7, before his cardiac arrest, are somehow the last of life that he will ever after know? What if the evident weakness of God with regard to this life (why not rid the world of Addison's disease?) extends also to life hereafter, and resting in God is nothing more than carrying on from where we left off in this life—a perpetual illness rather than healing?

The witness of faith in the resurrection is strong, yes, but it is not the only human witness to what happens after death. Stories of unhappy spirits abound. The belief in reincarnation is held by almost as many as those who believe in resurrection—the endless return of the soul to existence in a world of contingency, accident, illness, war, and death. Repeat it and repeat it.

And maybe the whole business is a chimera. Maybe, sadly, that was it: Thomas had sixteen years, many of them shadowed by unhappiness, and now it is over. C. S. Lewis is right: the worst is not to believe there is no god. The worst is to believe there *is* God, and now we have seen the true measure of this god and know to stay as far away as possible. But how to get away from God?

Journal Entry, September 3

Great dream about Alexis: She's gone off to New York University and has auditioned for a role in a big, important Broadway show—as big as *Cats* or *Les Miserables*. She gets the part—she is to play the fairy or angel who, at the end, flies way up high above the stage to put the star on the Christmas tree and say the last lines. She's beside herself with excitement, and I'm excited for her. It's a great break. My worry is that she will be two hundred feet above the stage with a (fallible?) harness on and no net beneath her.

Journal Entry, September 8, 2002, Meditation at the Service of Memory for Thomas

It has been a long journey these past two months, from July 8th—when Thomas's heart first stopped and the lives of his mother, sister, and I stopped also—until now. I hope you will forgive me if I take a moment to say, on behalf of Kate and Alexis, as well as myself, a word of gratitude for the way all of you have accompanied us on this journey—beloved family members, dear friends, colleagues, some of you people whom we have never met before—all present in various ways, both physically and in spirit, in prayer and in coffee breaks, over Thomas's recumbent body and over meals together during these past two months. We would not be as whole and as strong as we are, were it not for all of you. One of the gifts during the seven weeks of Thomas's passage is the assurance we have gained that we will always carry the love we shared with Thomas, just as the love we shared with Thomas will always carry us. In the same way, we will always carry the memory of your care and friendship and love, just as these things will carry us for many years to come. So thank you, and God bless you all.

It is a rare and difficult privilege, but a blessing nevertheless, for a father to see both the first breath his son draws in and the last breath his son exhales. I will always be grateful that I was present at Thomas's birth—when the doctor lifted him, wet and red, from his mother's womb after a cesarian section—and at his death—when our fair young man lay helpless before all that life had brought him and finally breathed his last. Birth, death—bookend moments of a life all too brief, while brimming with potential.

Several weeks before Thomas died, while he lay in hospice care, his mother and I were talking about the way it felt to be waiting—waiting for we weren't sure what. We knew by then what the end would be, just as in waiting for Thomas's birth we had known what we were waiting for. But of course we had not really known what all the labor leading to his birth would bring, any more than we knew what all the hard, exhausting work leading to the end of this long journey would finally bring. We are, in some ways, still waiting to see where our life with Thomas will take us, now that he has gone ahead of us.

Those weeks before his death all felt, oddly, a little like Advent, that period of weeks in the church calendar before Christmas—a time of preparation, of expectation, of introspection, of looking for something promised, though it may turn out to be not what we expected. So it seems appropriate to reflect on the way Advent is a period of hope and waiting. From our familiarity with the Christian story we know that Advent finally brings us to a birth which prefigures, through frankincense and myrrh, a meaningful death—a death which itself makes possible, in the end, another and transformative new birth.

T. S. Eliot, in "Journey of the Magi," writes of the way in which birth and death collapse into each other in the story of Jesus's Nativity. Birth and death together seen at once, so that the life of one human being can be comprehended, held together, and perhaps give new meaning to our waiting and our hoping.

A [hard] coming we had of it,
Just the worst time of year
For a journey, and such a long journey. . . .

All this was a long time ago, I remember,
And I would do it again, but set down
This set down
This: were we led all that way for
Birth or Death? There was a Birth, certainly,
We had evidence and no doubt. I had seen birth and death,
But had thought they were different; this Birth was
Hard and bitter agony for us, like Death, our death.
We returned to our places, these Kingdoms,
But no longer at ease here, in the old dispensation. . . .
I should be glad of another death.

After the long, arduous journey we have been on these past two months, we must somehow return to our places in the old dispensation—our work, our communities, our quotidian lives. But the old dispensation, the old way of life, will never be the same, and we will never be at ease as we were. My hope, my prayer, is that we will find in the memory of this time and the fellowship that held a young man at its center the grace and strength necessary for each day, through God's mercy.

Journal Entry, September 10, 2002

Today we had a second memorial service, this one at Emory for the many people who had been walking the journey with us but had been unable to attend the service two days ago.

One colleague said to me afterward, "This will sound wrong, but this has been a great experience." He meant not just the memorial service but the two months that preceded it. I knew what he meant—that in the throes of the hardest, coldest passages that many of us have ever had to make in life, we have been brought to the threshold of the great mystery of the greatest threshold, the one at the doorway that we cannot yet pass through until our time. We have stood at the doorway in wonder, fear, and awe. And we've been given a chance to look with close and unflinching attention at Thomas, at his passage that someday will perhaps provide a model for our own passage, and we have come to know our own hearts and their vulnerability.

What my colleague, John, meant was not that a premature death was something to celebrate, or even that the memorial service had been satisfying in some way. What he meant was that in the gathering of friends and strangers in prayer for a common end over the course of seven weeks, whether in the hospice room or in distant temples and churches, there had been through it all a sense of God having drawn near to succor, to comfort, to sustain, to deepen understanding, to strengthen bonds of friendship and family, to ease the dis-ease of being between the kingdom of earth and the kingdom of heaven, to forgive the unforgivable, and in the end to gather into God's great and ultimate being a beloved child of Our Father in Heaven. God had drawn close and had dwelt among us.

John had visited Thomas several times at the hospital and later in the hospice. The last time he came, I was sitting on one side of Thomas's bed, and his mother was on the other side, as several friends stood around us. It had felt, for an hour or more, as if Thomas might die at any moment.

All was quiet in the room, and I was holding Thomas's right hand. John came to stand behind me, and I reached over to pull a chair beside me and motion for John to sit. He did, and I took his hand and placed it over Thomas's. After about ten minutes, John rose and patted my shoulder. He was in tears as he left. Later in the afternoon he sent me an email apologizing for his blubbering: "I came to give you comfort and left an emotional mess. But I couldn't help thinking of my own son at that age and wondering how I would have gone on if I'd lost him."

Somehow John's comment after the memorial service—"this has been a great experience"—reminded me of something Oliver Wendell Holmes Jr. said about living through the fierceness of the Civil War: "The generation that carried on the war has been set apart by its experience. Through our great good fortune, in our youth our hearts were touched with fire. It was given to us to learn at the outset that life is a profound and passionate thing. . . . But, above all, we have learned that . . . the one and only success which it is [ours] to command is to bring to [our] work a mighty heart."

Thomas lingered for seven weeks because his own mighty heart would not stop beating. But his dying also set the stage for the community gathered around him to experience their own mighty heart. We were touched, if not by fire, then by depths of sorrow that broke our hearts, which likewise, somehow, miraculously, have kept on beating.

Journal Entry, September 21

One month since Thomas's death. Many people have told me that they have dreamed of him. I have not, though I long to see him vividly in a dream, smiling, healthy, happy. My mother told me that she had a dream about him two nights before he died. She dreamed that she and Dad were asleep in their bed when Thomas opened the door to their room and walked in without knocking. Startled, she sat up and looked at him. He was all dressed up, in a suit and tie, looking handsome. He announced, "I'm ready to go now, Grandma." She told me that she was certain they would receive a phone call that morning. Two days later he did go.

Journal Entry, November 1, All Saints Day

Kate and I have come to Green Bough House of Prayer, the little retreat center near the village of Adrian, Georgia, where I have often gone. It was the place where I had returned from on the Sunday that proved to be Thomas's last day of consciousness. We've come now with a holly tree and a small amount of Thomas's remaining ashes (the rest are in Decatur Cemetery, except for another small portion that Kate, Alexis, and I will take to New Orleans).

The golden afternoon is still and quiet in the crisp autumn coolness, the sort of day on which the sun's rays, slanting into the yellowing leaves of trees along the country highway, give one a sense of eternity just because of the obvious impermanence of all that is spread before us, which is timeless in its beauty, though carried away by time like all of us.

It's good to have such days to distract us from the horror of the memory of that morning of July 8th—the darkness of nighttime outside the emergency room entrance, the fatigue and fear that filled the waiting room, the appearance of Thomas's mother at the ICU room crying, anxious, momentarily confused and frustrated as she tried to find her way in through the curtain outside the glass wall of the room.

Those who try to offer encouragement by saying that Thomas lives on in our memories do not, in fact, offer much solace if that's the only eternal existence they can imagine. Not that I'm all that sure of much more. But if that's it, then, God, give me much more memory.

But I find that there are whole periods of his life for which I seem not to be able to remember very much, or in very much detail. Whole swaths of his existence are erased from my recollection. How is this possible—that I remember so little of my own life, and of my life with him from eight, nine, ten, twelve years ago? I was there every minute of it, it seemed, and yet it's vanished.

I remember helping him learn to ride his first two-wheel bike when he was five—doing it from the start without training wheels as I ran behind holding the seat to help him balance while he tooled around the parking lot of a bank near our house.

I remember helping Thomas, age seven or eight, clean the little bowl in which his goldfish, Jaws, swam, and when Jaws finally died, I remember going with Thomas and Alexis and their mother to bury the little fish in the back yard.

I remember trying to encourage Thomas to hang in with his Little League team when he wanted to give up on baseball at age ten or eleven, but he was always more interested in spending the time between innings going down to the creek behind the baseball fields to look for frogs.

I remember looking at him in the dentist's office when he was twelve, waiting for the consultation on what it would take to put braces on his teeth, and suddenly seeing that he was about to become an adolescent. The leanness of his face and a tilt of his head suggested a boy in transit from childhood to the burdens of teenhood. And I loved him for the innocence he was about to lose and for the angst he was about to begin carrying.

I remember him again at age five spilling his juice at the dinner table and saying, "Oh, dammit." When I asked him sternly what he had just said, he looked at me sheepishly and said, "I meant, God dammit"—as if adding God's name here would redeem the error. No doubt it did. Everyone at the table had a good laugh. And I vowed to curb my own tongue around him.

I walked outside after night prayer to the spot where, earlier this evening, we planted an East Palatka holly and buried some of Thomas's ashes. Stars in the sky like I had not seen them in a long time—numerous beyond numbering, speckling the blackness with white. All the clichés about human insignificance in perspective still are true. Thomas in the cold ground, the chilly fall air getting under my jacket. My poor, poor boy.

Yet there is a feeling of persisting spirit. How?

Journal Entry, November 21

How did they go on—those infinitely numerous mothers and fathers who watched their sons go off to war but waited in vain for them to return? Mothers who watched helplessly as their sickly infants failed to flourish and gradually wasted away. Fathers whose sons and daughters died from starvation, burning, drowning, falling, murder, choking, typhoid, smallpox, pneumonia, polio, cancer, measles, bee stings, snake bites, attacks by wild animals, flu, rabies, malformed hearts, cystic fibrosis—Addison's!

Journal Entry, November 22

One more indignity for Thomas, as if all the indignities inflicted by the ICU and hospice were not enough. The manager of the cemetery where his ashes (mostly) are buried botched the plaque with his name and dates. He just arbitrarily decided that since Thomas's entire name, Thomas John Anthony Hauk, could not fit on one line, the plaque would read only Thomas John Hauk. No consulting, no questions, no phone call to see if that would be all right. Lord, God! I insisted that he correct the mistake, and that the entirety of my son's identity be presented to the world as long as the cemetery endures.

Journal Entry, November 23

I am on a two-week solo journey to drive through the wintriest parts of my soul as well as the wintriest parts of the country. I have flown to Harrisburg, Pennsylvania, for a brief visit with family before renting a car to drive up through the center of the state, into western New York and across the Adirondacks into New England. Along the way I've stopped in Ithaca, Syracuse, and Lake Placid, New York (where I picked up a cold); Hanover, New Hampshire. Snow had fallen deep across New York.

I am now in Bangor, Maine, where I had breakfast at a place called Geaghain's. The waiter was a lad—a high school kid named Trevor, clean-faced with a good, up-to-date haircut, eager to make sure I had enough coffee. In his diligence, he reminded me of Thomas conscientiously busing tables at Urban Cannibals, the sandwich shop down the street from where we lived. Tevor had Thomas's spirit, it seemed—a similar winsome and wholesome way of lighting the wintry morning with his presence. One gets a sense, from such encounters, of how Jesus's followers might have seen his spirit moving among them in the days after his death—the kindness of a stranger, the camaraderie over a shared meal, the insight of a teacher or fellow-disciple sounding an echo of the Master.

My brain, though, is disintegrating. Lying in bed, waiting for sleep, I carry on an imaginary argument with a professor I've known for a decade, but at the summation, as I'm driving home the clinching point, I can't remember his last name! Eventually it comes, but whatever happened to "the tip of my tongue"? The tip of my tongue seems to have become as empty as my head.

And I imagine death all around. I worry that Alexis will lose another male family member—perhaps one of her grandfathers, or me!—before the month is out. I wonder how she would fare at losing two, three, or four of the most significant males of her childhood within a few months of each other? This is strange, and yet it is not beyond possibility.

Weird images float in front of my eyes when my eyelids close in the dark—not the usual moiré and paisley patterns but odd little creatures, like hobbits but smaller, engaged in activity of various kinds. It must be the effects of my cold or the medicine I'm taking for it.

Journal Entry, November 24

Not much sleep last night, and more fatigue from the seven hours of driving from Castine, Maine, to Amherst, Massachusetts. In the motel I watched a little of *Mouse Hunt*. I don't know whether Thomas ever saw it, but I can imagine him enjoying the slapstick of it and the holiday air. It's the sort of show he and Alexis would have lain around watching in their matching red long johns when they were small. Such a weight, all day, of feeling that the past is lost—the happier, taken-for-granted mundaneness of life all gone. Of course, it's not lost, exactly. It's just past—over—and no longer to be reminisced about in the presence of "The Boy," as Alexis often called him. I can't help thinking that he is with us even so. Sometimes. Somehow.

Journal Entry, November 25

Remembering Thomas as he lay there in final stillness for an hour after death, as the hospice staff gave us time alone until it was, finally, time for them to do their work. The image of him— almost skeletal, reminding me of Auschwitz corpses—led me to imagine what it would have been like to have been forced, shorn, naked, and cold, into a chamber with my sixteen-year-old son and other men and boys to await the inevitable. What thoughts. How to rid myself of them.

Journal Entry, November 26

I feel that I have gained no wisdom in the past three months. I have been pushed very hard to wonder about the Divine and its power, or rather its apparent powerlessness. Like Mark Twain in his later years, I feel estranged from God. Nor am I certain I want to call a truce, though I doubt that I have a choice.

How will we all be gathered into God's presence at the end? Will we be?

It's possible to see the lasting significance of the greats—the way a great author or scientist or leader changes the consciousness and the memory of humankind for generations. That is a kind of discernible immortality, though I wonder if the greats in their tombs know anything about it.

But what of the rest of us? Yes, we may change life (for good or ill) for some of those who are immediately around us. But beyond a small circle of friends and family, what?

Are we like the putative butterfly wing in Japan whose flutter changes the weather in England according to some metaphors of quantum physics? And do we thus have some world-shaping impact that we will never know anything about? Are we all George Baileys who need a guardian angel to show us the unguessed-at good that we have done, or the unimagined bad that would have happened if we had not been here?

I guess I'm looking here for some meaning to my own life as well as to Thomas's.

Journal Entry, November 29

Thanksgiving gathering yesterday at Mom and Dad's house in Pennsylvania with siblings, in-laws, nieces, nephews, a great rambunctious bunch. I feel more mute than ever among people, as if my brain can no longer function even as slowly as it used to on a normal day. I have to reach for names, for common words. I seem grossly inarticulate in ordinary conversation, able to talk about only what is directly in front of me—the football game, the food on the table, the weather. I'm conscious of how much, in the past nineteen years, I've relied on my children as the source of something to talk about, and of how much I allow my conversations to be directed by my interlocutors; I depend on them to offer up the topics or respond to my questions.

Writing has become just a way of recording what passes through the day, keeping it all from evaporating completely from memory.

Alexis called the other day and left a sweet voice message. She said she had heard from one of her professors (maybe her English professor, whom I know well and have been in touch with) that I was feeling a little under the weather, and that she felt like she hadn't talked to me in a long time, and that she loved me lots. She sounded a little teary. She is a precious, fragile soul, more special and rare than she fully knows.

Journal Entry, November 30

Sitting in BWI Airport waiting to board a plane for home, I'm aware of a boy—maybe two or three years old—who's fussing about having to sit patiently in this place that offers so little for him. The seats are hard, the air is chilly, the noise is oppressive, the crowds press in. It all bothers me, so why would it not bother him? His parents—thirty-something and well dressed—are absorbed in each other and ignoring him until his insistence (Daddy! Daddy!) gets the attention of the father, who leans around the mother and swats the boy on the leg. Once. Twice. Still the boy fusses. Dad gets up and steps to the boy, puts his face into his son's, and says, "Next time it'll be harder. Much harder."

I think how much the dad might choose to redo that moment if he knew the son would be with him only until midnight.

Journal Entry, February 16

Maybe all spirituality is merely reducible to biochemistry of the brain. We see the universe in a certain way—we have faith in a higher being, we hope for an afterlife—because the mix of molecules through our brain inclines us that way, while another person's different brain mix inclines them not to have that faith or hope.

On the other hand, the spirit may be, in fact, more than or other than the body, more than the firing of neurons in the cerebral cortex.

Thomas in his coma seemed to suggest both possibilities but proved neither. If the spirit that animated him was only the workings of his brain, why does his spirit still seem to inhabit my days? But if his spirit was somehow more than the workings of the body, why does the absence of his body so diminish the poignant sense of his spirit? There is something about the spirit-animated body that makes the whole person. Thomas's body with a dormant spirit was not him; Thomas's spirit, wherever it is, without his body is not him. The "he" that I called Thomas is gone.

Journal Entry, March 8

How indeed is it possible that Thomas ever was? By that I mean that life seems to have continued so fully, so indifferently without him, that I have to stretch memory and imagination to feel that there was a reality that was him. When each of us is gone from the world, how quickly the world will go on living and working as if we had never been here, as if we'd never mattered to anyone.

Oh, my son—to have paid attention more acutely; to have loved more patiently; to have fathered more intently.

Journal Entry, April 19

My botanist friend Carl and I were talking about the large, old Japanese magnolia that stands at the edge of the Emory University Quadrangle. He believes it to be one of the largest of its species in the state. Certainly it's been standing there just as large as it is for as long as I've been at Emory, and probably much longer—possibly since at least the 1960s.

It usually blooms in late February, glorious in its mauve and pink splendor. But once in a while it gets caught by a late freeze when its blossoms are already in full bloom. Once, for instance, a blizzard hit on March 13 and froze all the blossoms, turning them brown and leaving a sodden mess on the ground after they all fell off the tree.

Carl said that when that kind of shock to the system happens, the tree dies back a little, and the next year it doesn't flower as gloriously as the previous year. It's as if the tree has a visceral memory of the previous year's trauma and chooses caution over impetuous flowering. It will ease into life gingerly this time, risking less.

This may be a metaphor for the soul. In the wake of trauma, the soul, too, can close in on itself and take great care, lest another shock prove too much and completely undo it. The bromide we sometimes hear is that what doesn't kill us will make us stronger. We graciously and hopefully assert that life sometimes prunes us with adversity so that we can blossom more fully. But I don't think that's necessarily true. Sometimes the pruning is not the work of a master arborist carefully and judiciously trimming just the right branches. Rather, sometimes it is the ravaging of a chainsaw cutting at our roots.

Journal Entry, Holy Saturday, April 19

Last month, in Lent, the weekend after Mardi Gras, I drove with Alexis and Kate and a college friend of Alexis's to New Orleans with some of Thomas's ashes. We spent a day wandering the French Quarter and eating food that Thomas would have loved. The sky was the color of a gray tabby cat, and a light drizzle fell almost continuously as we sheltered under umbrellas and stayed close to the buildings while we walked. Debris lay here and there in the streets as reminders of the celebrations earlier in the week—a few strings of Mardi Gras beads in the gutters, piles of trash swept up in alleys for collection, odds and ends of clothing lying about.

On our second day we walked the several blocks from our hotel to Jackson Square. At Café du Monde we had beignets and café au lait. Thomas and I had gone there twice on our first visit to the city. On our second visit to the café we picked up beignets and frozen café au lait to go before we caught a cab for the train station and our rail trip home. Now, as light rain fell, Kate, Alexis, Gabi, and I looked out onto Jackson Square, the park across the street, and knew where to leave the ashes we were carrying.

Finishing our breakfast, we walked across Decatur Street to the entrance to Jackson Square and circled back along the inside of the fence toward the corner where Decatur Street meets St. Anne Street. There, a small grove of trees sheltered a cluster of large azalea bushes directly catty-corner from Café du Monde. I found a stick and crawled my way in under the azaleas, where I scratched out a little trough. The women stood guard, reminding me of the women at the tomb on Easter Sunday. No resurrection here. I poured the handful of ashes into the trough and covered it up, then broke the stick in two to make a little cross, which I laid atop the newly turned dirt. A part of

Thomas will always remain in the city that most enchanted him.

As we stood to leave, the sky suddenly brightened, and after two days of sodden weather, the sun appeared. The moment could not have been more of a Hollywood cliché. But it happened. Sun beaming down as if on the happy finale to a story of fear and sorrow. Except that it was still not a happy finale.

Talking yesterday with my friend Lynnsay about the "dark night of the soul," I mentioned the company I have been keeping—John of the Cross, Thérèse of Lisieux, Mother Teresa. Thérèse's yearning to know and see the suffering of Jesus prompted me to say that I found such longing odd. I wasn't sure that my faith led me to yearn for Jesus as a companion. I just am not sure what that would mean. Lynnsay said it didn't matter, because I had experienced that suffering in knowing the dying of Thomas, who has become a kind of Christ to me—a forerunner in the kingdom and an advocate.

When she suggested that I try to picture Thomas with God, I said that "heaven" doesn't work for me in that respect: nothing like *The Lovely Bones* and loved ones watching us from beyond. What does help is the iconographic tradition of the church—the ascended Christ at God's right hand, Thomas at God's side. Images I've seen of Christ with his hands raised in priestly blessing and thumbs and index fingers forming a circle—in a pose similar to that of the meditating Buddha, the meditating Thomas.

I now have a sense that I can call on Thomas to help me, to be present with me through the hours—the days, weeks, months, years—that will make up whatever time remains to me in this life, which seems overwhelmingly burdensome in its potential length. How best to fill the hours is the question—what to do, what to do. I suppose that the answer will be revealed.

Speaking of revelation, Lynnsay said that the sun's coming out in New Orleans immediately after we left some of Thomas's ashes under an azalea bush at Jackson Square was for her a revelation: a signal that Thomas is okay.

I'm not convinced that I can read the same meaning into the moment. I'm not convinced that I will see him again. I am like the Apostle Thomas doubting reports of Jesus's appearance after the crucifixion.

But I am prepared for anything.

Meditation One: Out of a Dead Tree

A shoot will come up from the stump of Jesse;
from his roots a Branch will bear fruit.
—Isaiah 11:1 (NIV)

Most of us can never forget our one great grief and the way the pain of it nearly tore us apart. Whatever the cause of that grief was, it was a death. The death of love perhaps. The loss of hope; the loss of meaning. All those things. Some of us bear many more than one such grief. We remember, though, don't we? How could we forget?

Of course all the old clichés are true: time heals; life goes on; activity mends sorrow.

But, no—you will never again have back that living thing that died; that love; that marriage; that child; that parent; that friendship; that sense of achievement; that open horizon of possibility. That feeling is gone. And, worse, the source of that feeling, the thing that generated joy, is gone forever. It is dead and gone. No chance of bringing it back. Not even a chance of finding out where it went, so that you could track it down and breathe your own breath into it, try CPR.

It's something of what Israel must have felt in the days of Isaiah. The kingdom was destroyed, the future foreclosed, God apparently absent, the promise of an enduring relationship over. How do you get God back? You might as well ask how to make the days longer as the sun declines in December. Or how to make the rain stop when it shows no sign of letting up after days. Or how to bring life to a lifeless stump—to a fence post.

A few weeks after Thomas died, we planted an overcup oak, *Quercus lyrata,* in his memory on the Emory Quadrangle. That was in early September. That autumn the leaves on the tree died and fell along with all the leaves on the larger, older, mightier trees on the Quad, and the little bare tree passed through the winter. I looked forward to spring and the tree's revival.

Sure enough, as Shakespeare says, "time will bring on summer, and thistles will have leaves as well as thorns, and be as sweet as sharp." Time brought on springtime in Atlanta, a glorious profusion of dogwoods, azaleas, forsythia, gardenia, and countless blossoms that spread their pollen everywhere. But while all around the Quadrangle flowers bloomed and bushes greened and buds and leaves filled the trees, the little overcup oak stood bare. By Holy Week it was the sole unadorned collection of sticks in sight, barren as a pile of kindling. Despite my daily visits and exhortations for the little tree to break forth in greenery, it remained bare and brown.

In due course Easter came. That Sunday afternoon, late in the day, I went for a run through the campus and found my way leading to the tree. Stopping to examine it, I looked as closely for signs of life as human eyes could look. Here, to my mind, were branches dead for certain. Dead as a chair leg. Frustratingly so. Grief-makingly so.

Unbidden and unlooked for came to me the first line of a Dylan Thomas poem, "The Force that Through the Green Fuse Drives the Flower." Some force was necessary to drive through the brown branches the greening of this tree. Wishing would not make it so. It was beyond my power, utterly. Not a thing I could do.

"It's up to you, Thomas," I whispered: "Drive the green force through these branches. Make them sprout." And I ran on.

Next morning, walking across the Quad to my office, I stopped at the Thomas tree. And there, astonishingly, were tiny leaves popping out all over, no more than an eighth of an inch long at this point, mere promises of green to come, but unmistakably real. The tree was beginning to leaf. It was, to me, the kind of coincidence—dare one say miracle?—that makes you want to laugh. In a movie it would be the cause for a critic's ridicule: implausible, hokey, contrived. And yet, there those little buds were.

Now the rest of the story is less cinematically happy. That tree flourished for a time, but the summer heat wore on it, and insects bored into it, and just after Thomas's seventeenth birthday in July, it died, never to be revived. Thomas's mother remarked that he would have laughed to think of the tree being bored to death at the university.

The kind and generous groundskeeping department, which so beautifully maintains the Emory campus, removed the dead tree and planted in its place a Nuttall's oak, *Quercus texana*—named for another Thomas, the English botanist Thomas Nuttall.

I do remember my own great griefs. I understand that what has been lost will never again be present to me. Of course I do.

Nevertheless, the prophet Isaiah promises that this life of loss and death is being made new. Can I believe it? I know that the stump of Jesse is an old, useless stump—like the source of my grief, a dead piece of tree that reminds me of good days gone by. But, oh—had I but eyes to see and grace to understand. For out of that dry dead thing is coming something new. Can I begin to see it?

Meditation Two: What Lasts

T. S. Eliot remarks in "East Coker" that "As we grow older / The world becomes stranger, the pattern more complicated / Of dead and living." The complications come in many forms and from many surprising directions—births, deaths, new friendships, lost friendships, illness, healing, responsibilities, irresponsibilities. The stories about these complications often touch our hearts with pain—from which, as Aeschylus knew, "comes wisdom through the awful grace of God."

One such story of complication, pain, wisdom, and grace is the book of Tobit, part of the Apocrypha in many bibles. Tobit is a bit like Job, a righteous man who has sought to obey God and help all who are in need, but who nevertheless suffers grave misfortune. When he and his family, along with many other Israelites, are taken into exile by the Assyrians, Tobit continues to live according to the commands of God. His faithfulness to his religion earns the respect of the emperor, Shalmaneser, who entrusts him with great responsibilities. Tobias becomes wealthy but continues to live righteously.

Through a series of misfortunes, however, Tobit becomes blind and unable to work. Life becomes "stranger, more complicated." Poverty looms. He feels anguish for his wife and son, who have descended into dire circumstances because of Tobit's fate. Why has this calamity befallen him? We are not told. But his profound misery leads him to pray to God to let him die and end his suffering.

Awaiting death, Tobit recalls that when he was wealthy, he buried some treasure in a distant town. He wants his family to have it after he's gone, so he sends his son, Tobias, to fetch it. When he reaches the town where the treasure is buried, Tobias meets Sarah. This unfortunate woman is cursed by a demon bent on killing anyone she marries. Seven times she has married, but each time, the demon has killed her husband. For her, life has become strange and complicated indeed.

Why has she been cursed in this way? We are not told. In despair, Sarah, too, prays to God to end her suffering.

The story of Tobit seems to be designed, in part, to teach us that the personal travails of one human being are not inconsequential to God. For in the story God hears the prayers of Tobit and Sarah and answers them—not by granting what they ask for, which is death. No, God has compassion on the sufferings of his people and sends an angel, Raphael, to make things right again. With Raphael's help, Tobias defeats the demon and marries Sarah. Through the miraculous ministrations of Raphael, Tobit's sight and fortunes are restored, and he lives for another five decades. After a long and prosperous life, Tobit dies at peace.

But if the lesson is that God hears our prayers, what are we to make of the dissonance we may feel between this story and our own lives? How do we explain the often apparent lack of response to our own prayers for healing, for cure, for strong limbs in place of atrophied, or for mental tranquility in place of mental illness? We are often at a loss for what to say in the face of the child dying of cancer, the young woman made blind by neurological disease, the boy given a limp for the rest of his life because of polio. Do we dare to pray for their restoration to a full and vibrant life?

What we know from the story of Tobit is that even the healthy die at last, as the healed Tobit does. In fact, the death of Tobit reminds me of *The Last Temptation of Christ*, the great novel by the Greek writer Nikos Kazantzakis. In that book, we encounter Lazarus after Jesus has raised him from the dead. It is not a condition—this resurrection life—that Lazarus finds particularly worth having. Enervated, laconic, surprised by his waking from what felt like a dream, he can barely engage with those around him. He somewhat resents having been brought back to endure once again the slings and arrows of human existence. Asked which is better, life or death, he replies, "Six of one, half a dozen of the other." And, in the end, he dies again, this time brutally done in by none other than Barabbas, the criminal who is chosen to be set free by the crowd that sends Jesus to his death. So, yes—life can bring healing, but there will still be, inevitably, death.

There is good news, though. For along the way, according to the story of Tobit, there is the grace of divine companionship, often, like Raphael, in disguise, unrecognized. Along the way we will learn amazing things if we keep our ears and eyes attuned to the world (the guts of a fish have restorative and magical powers; who knew?). And along the way our lives will always be nothing more nor less than an unmerited gift, enriching us in ways that we will become aware of only in a future that we cannot imagine (just as Tobias's wealth and Sarah's marriage and Tobit's healing all seem to have been prepared without their knowledge).

It is worth noting, though, that the healing that takes place in the story of Tobit does not erase the suffering and loss that precede it. Yes, Sarah's demon is destroyed, and she's able to live a long and happy married life. True, the scales on Tobit's eyes fall away, and he regains his sight. But loss and blessing are two sides of the same coin or the same life, as are suffering and triumph. The joy of restored sight cannot be known without the earlier blindness. "Happily ever after" does not come before great trial and difficulty.

My own story of loss is also one of blessing, one that continues to touch me deeply.

That night when I woke from a dream to find that my son was dying. That call to 911, CPR, the bursting in of the emergency medical technicians just minutes later—the frenzy to try to bring this child back from the brink of death, or even from death itself. I was convinced that Thomas had died. And yet I prayed, "God Almighty – you brought your own son back from the dead, bring back my son also." By the time the ambulance crew carried Thomas on a stretcher downstairs, the damage to his brain was irreparable, and Thomas began a seven-week, comatose decline leading to his eventual death.

Throughout his journey, he was surrounded by prayer, and prayers rose from around the world for his recovery, his wakening to new life, and his eventual healing. And yet, what would it mean to find healing in such a situation? Could missing brain tissue be restored? Could memory function that had been erased ever be replaced? Could that spirit that seemed to have left the body ever be brought back? No. No. No.

All of us will die. Of course we know that, however much we distract ourselves from the knowledge. Tobit died; Tobias died; Sarah died; Thomas died.

What lasts, on the other hand, is the spirit that accompanied them on their way. What lasts is the spirit that accompanies us on our way. Raphael, the messenger of the divine, the companion on our journey, is the assurance that we can live "as if" we are already healed—as if our life has no struggle, as if no demon threatens our wedding night, as if we will not wander until the end of our days without sufficient sight or adequate light to see where we are going. The role of the Spirit—in whatever way we think of the Spirit—is to carry us along regardless of the outcome from our prayer. The healing of our lives comes from that Spirit.

If anyone protests that this is an unsatisfying, spiritualized view of disease and healing, an insufficient and ghostly answer to hard concrete reality, we might recall the words of Jesus: Is it more difficult to cure the sick or to forgive? To paraphrase, is it more difficult to cure the illness of the body or to heal the broken spirit, to mend disjointed relationships, to regather a scattered community, to bring peace to a warring world?

For me, as Thomas lingered, Raphael came in the guise of the community who walked with me and Thomas's family through the long ordeal of his dying. In a sense, God did grant my plea that night. Thomas, who seemed surely gone from us when the ambulance arrived, nevertheless came back long enough for true healing to begin—healing of Thomas's family and community. Raphael, the messenger of God, arrived in the form of scores of friends and strangers, of the intermingled fellowship of love and compassion that surrounded Thomas's bed.

Raphael is found also in the communities who minister in countless ways through our own lives—the hands and feet of Christ in the world. More than this, the story of Tobit and Tobias tells us how to avail ourselves of the Spirit by experiencing community as the means of grace. Tobit needs Tobias, as Tobias needs Raphael, as Sarah needs Tobias. Tobit is the story of how to live into grace by developing the habits of faith and prayer, of love and hope, of reliance on others. These are not a recipe for a pain-free life. They are a means, a practice, for spirit-enlivened existence, for being open to the healing and holy mystery of God in the world.

The experience of Thomas's passing—and other moments of tragedy, foolishness, and loss in my life—persuade me that there is a mystery whose power we see glimpses of, and whose efficacy we don't fully understand, but whose sureness we can be grateful for when our deepest hopes are fulfilled. And when those hopes are not satisfied—as they were not in Thomas's case—we have the company of angels and all the saints of heaven and earth. In this lies healing.

We have all heard stories about or known someone or been ourselves the person who experienced a miracle: the cancer, usually fatal, that goes into remission after prayer; the disease that has resisted every medical art and scientific ministration but succumbs, strangely and coincidentally, to the words and ritual of the healing rite in the prayer book; the afflicted mind that gives way to the explainable but still wondrous power of pharmaceutical therapy. Is there a difference between the shaman's burning of certain flowers or animal parts and the blocking of serotonin in neural synapses by selective serotonin reuptake inhibitors? I can explain one scientifically and not the other. I can't say that I understand the source of the effectiveness of either.

All we can do—if we are persons of faith, and maybe even if we are not—is to accede to the truth of our eyes and our experience and say that some authority governs the outcome of our lives. And this, in the end, is what Tobit is most clearly about: acknowledging that what is most necessary is not so much healing *by* the Spirit, with a capital S, as healing *of* our *own* spirits. It is about the ease of existential pain that comes from recognizing that all we have, all we are, and all we ever will be is a gift from whatever creative being wrought our lives.

The marriage of Sarah to Tobias is incidental to the healing of her despair, it does not cause that healing. The recovery of sight by Tobit is incidental to the healing of his broken spirit, it is not what heals his spirit. What really *heals* them, in the most profound way, is their recognition of the truth to which Tobit gives voice in chapter 13. I paraphrase verse 6:

Turn to God with all your heart and soul and mind
and live in truth.
Then will God turn his face upon you,
and make himself known to you again.
Remember all that God has done for you,
and give thanks with a loud voice.
Bless the Lord, who is righteous forever.

I give thanks that my troubled and despairing spirit has been so often surrounded by a cloud of witnesses to the power of God's Spirit, the power to chase away demons. I give thanks that the community in which I found myself so long ago could open my eyes to see the One who gives us life and light. And I give thanks that as those with whom I journey—and those with whom everyone journeys—share our burdens with each other, we might be for one another the angels in disguise that God means us to be.

Epilogue

It certainly seems true, as Hemingway observed, that "the world breaks everyone." Live long enough (which for many is not very long), and you will suffer the indignities and abuses of the human condition. I am not sure, though, that it necessarily follows, as he thought, that "many are strong at the broken places." It's a manly thing to say. The broken places—the fractured, torn, and scarred parts of ourselves—may knit back together, and that repair work may suggest a certain resilience. We do go on until we don't. But like the stigmata of the risen Jesus, the evidence of wounding remains. Sometimes so does the pain. Like the phantom pain that can exist where an amputated arm or leg no longer is, soul pain can linger or reassert itself long after the loss of a loved one. So it has been since Thomas's passing.

Often, when I meet someone for the first time, they ask whether I have children. This question is not difficult to answer. Yes, I say: I have a daughter who is grown and married and making her way as a writer and theater critic, and I had a son who died two decades ago when he was sixteen. Sometimes I sense that while the answer is easy to deliver, the second part is difficult for the questioner to receive. It takes a moment for them to process my response and shift to the unexpected need to express sympathy. At other times, though, I hear a story offered, as if in solidarity, about the questioner's own loss of a spouse or a child, and I realize again that the world breaks everyone. We all have broken places.

When Thomas was thirteen, he was enamored of the strong men throwing each other around in the world of professional wrestling. Perhaps because he was newly weakened by Addison's disease, he saw in those men both something to admire and something to define himself over against. He wrote a poem:

Strength

Is strength for only strong men, wrestlers, or boxers?
I don't know, but I think it goes farther.
Strength means sticking with something.
Strength means living through hard times.
Strength means not giving up.
Who is really strong?
I like to think I am.
Are you?

EPILOGUE

If there is one word that I would use to describe Thomas these many years after his death, it is that word "strength." Besides being the title of his poem, it is the one word in addition to his first name that's on his grave marker in the Decatur cemetery. He admired people with not only physical strength, but moral strength as well, and the ability to live fearlessly in the face of the ambiguity of life. He was fortunate to meet two great moral exemplars when he was twelve years old — the Dalai Lama and Archbishop Desmond Tutu. I like to think that Thomas, like those two Nobel peace laureates, found strength in his ability to connect with people out of his curiosity and compassion, his interest in who they were and how they lived, and his hope for common ground.

More than four hundred and fifty people filled the church where we held his first memorial service. The gathering music included the song "Sons," from *Jacques Brel Is Alive and Well and Living in Paris.* Thomas's mother somehow courageously sang it.

Eight Tibetan Buddhist monks from Drepung Loseling Monastery chanted a prayer in their native language, their multiphonic throat singing filling the space with a sound evocative of mystery. Thomas's sister read a poem, "Ode to a Bumblebee," by Pablo Neruda because the light and color and sprightliness of the verse evoked for her the spirit of her brother. For the boy who charmed and was beloved by women, women clergy took a prominent part: an Episcopal priest prayed the invocation, a Methodist minister offered a meditation, and a distinguished biblical scholar delivered the closing benediction—all women. For the young man who had won the hearts of men, a Baptist minister gave the eulogy, a Congregationalist minister prayed, and a Black Baptist preacher lifted up the spirit of Thomas in a ritual of returning him to God. A group of five women sang "I'll Fly Away" to close the service, and the final organ music was a light, airy improvisation on Beethoven's "Ode to Joy."

Two days later an equal number filled Cannon Chapel at Emory University in a service for that community. Afterward, we filed onto the Quadrangle and planted that overcup oak that would not last a year but would be replaced by a Nuttall's oak. After the gathered community recited a brief liturgy, a bagpiper played "Amazing Grace," and people drifted away by twos and threes. A student I knew approached me with tears streaming down her face and handed me a beautifully painted clay pot in which she had placed seeds: rue for sorrow, rosemary for remembrance, lily for sweet innocence.

And then his mother, sister, and I gathered one morning with a friend and the Episcopal priest to commit Thomas's ashes, or most of them, into the ground in the cinerarium of the Decatur city cemetery. A foot-square marble plaque is set into the earth above his ashes. The plaque is inscribed with his first name and the Japanese character for "strength."

EPILOGUE

These many years later the spirit of Thomas continues to play among us. As a friend wrote in an email while Thomas lay in a coma, "Even as Thomas has slept . . . , he has deeply changed and opened the hearts of many people. He still has gifts to give." I feel the gift of his life daily, even as I miss his presence with every new experience that I wish I could share with him.

Following the suggestion of friends who had lost their teenage daughter to cancer just a few months before Thomas died, his mother and I established a scholarship in his memory through the Decatur Education Foundation. With the help of many friends and continued contributions through the years, the scholarship has underwritten part of the continuing education for nearly two dozen young men and women who have graduated from Decatur High School and gone on to college.

That Nuttall's oak that we planted in Thomas's memory on the Emory Quadrangle, the oak a symbol of strength, continues to flourish and has become tall with an expansive, magnificent canopy. It is usually the first tree on the Quad to bud in the spring and the last to lose its leaves in the fall. The leaves hang on well into winter. They hang on strong—even at the places where they are dying. Strength.

Acknowledgments

I owe thanks for the title of this book to my friend and mentor Jon Gunnemann, emeritus professor of social ethics in the Candler School of Theology at Emory University. During a visit to the hospital while Thomas was in the ICU, Jon and I stepped away to the cafeteria for a cup of coffee and conversation. As we talked, he pointed me to an essay in the book *Real Presences* by the philosopher George Steiner. That essay concludes with Steiner's extended reflection on the in-betweenness of Holy Saturday, a period of ambiguity that in Steiner's view has impelled much of the cultural richness of the past two millennia of human history. I'm grateful to Jon for his suggestion to pick up Steiner's book. It was Jon, too, who encouraged me to resume the project after more than twenty years. "There's only one reason why you should write it," he said, "and that's because you want to."

Several long-time friends read and commented on earlier drafts of the book. William M. Chace, president emeritus of Emory and a gifted prose stylist as well as an insightful literary critic and dear friend, read with great care and offered suggestions that improved whatever artistry the book contains. Ron Sauder, himself a superb writer as well as a book publisher and expert in communications, provided initial encouragement when I was uncertain that the book was worth seeing in print. I'm grateful to him and his Secant Publishing for bringing the book to the public. John Witte Jr.—an eminent scholar and extraordinary friend, whose own many books fill the shelves of libraries around the world—responded to an early draft with generous and thoughtful comments that kept me going. W. Clyde Partin Jr., MD, a master clinician and distinguished emeritus professor of medicine at Emory University School of Medicine, offered helpful insight into Addison's disease and, himself a writer, read the entire manuscript with a keen eye.

Thomas's mother, Kate Hauk, and his sister, Alexis Victoria Hauk, read and commented on the final draft. They, more than anyone else, know the trauma and burden of that summer so long ago. I am ever grateful for their love for Thomas and each other, and for their sharing with me their insights into the different ways they experienced Thomas's passing. Their perspectives, while not a part of this work, nevertheless enrich my understanding of that time.

Sara Haigh Hauk has been my wife and partner now since 2005. She met Thomas the year before he died and, like so many, was enchanted by his humor, hospitality, and interest in her. She helped him bleach his hair and went with us to professional sports events and movies; he in turn explained to her his father's impatience about many things. By coincidence, she had stopped by his hospice room on the evening of his last day, and as it became clear that something about his breathing had changed, she stood by me as he faded from us over the course of several hours, his respiration diminishing by degrees. Nearly every year since his passing, she and I have run a 5K race that raises money for the Decatur Education Foundation and, in our case, specifically for the Thomas Hauk Memorial Scholarship. I am daily blessed by Sara Haigh's love, companionship, insight, and wisdom.

For all those who offered consolation, friendship, food, tears, and even laughter in that dark time, I give thanks always. Some of them appear anonymously in these pages as writers of emails. Others who wrote emails, letters, notes, and cards are held in my memory forever. All of them are part of the great company of saints, living and dead, who sing with longing for the day when "God shall wipe away all tears from their eyes; and there shall be no more death, neither sorrow, nor crying." Even so, Lord, quickly come.

About the Author

A writer, editor, ethicist, and historian, Gary S. Hauk worked with four Emory University presidents as vice president and secretary of the university and later as deputy and then senior adviser to the president. He earned BA and MA degrees in English literature as well as a divinity degree and a PhD in Christian ethics. Since retiring from Emory in January 2020, he has continued to work as a freelance editor and writer and frequently preaches in Episcopal churches.